Mandy Johnston

JOHNSTON
ASSOCIATES
INTERNATIONAL

P.O. BOX 313
MEDINA, WASHINGTON 98039
(206) 454-7333

Stepping Out in Seattle, First Edition

ISBN: 1-881409-03-1

The listings and information appearing in this edition were current at the time of the final editing, but are subject to change at any time. No gratuities of any kind have been solicited or accepted from listed firms.

First printing November, 1992
cover art and book design by Mike Jaynes
Production by Kate Perrett and Ed Hochart

JASI
Post Office box 313
Medina, Washington 98039 U.S.A.
206-454-7333

Printed in the United States of America
Distributed in Canada by Raincoast Books Ltd.

Table of Contents

Introduction

When I researched and wrote this book, I had one important purpose in mind. I wanted to help solve the riddle of "What do you want to do tonight?" "I don't know, what do *you* want to do?" In pursuit of the perfect answers to this age-old question, I interviewed both men and women, ages eighteen to sixty-plus. Then I personally visited each suggested location. I spoke with hostesses, waiters, managers, and bartenders. I interviewed ticket takers and publicists, strangers in the crowd and friends of friends. Every entry in this book has been recommended and double checked, either by me or by my fellow authors. I think it's more than safe to say this is a "couple-tested," "friends-tested" guidebook.

Now, I can't promise you'll have the perfect date or day together, but I can suggest that you can follow in the well-trod paths of others and use this book to answer the question: "What do you want to do?" For the sake of a new, old, or yet-to-be-begun relationship, I hope that you enjoy romantic candlelit dinners, a wild and woolly day of shopping together, Salsa dancing or chamber music, whatever turns you on!

My many contributors and fellow authors know that we have only scratched the surface of things to do and places to go in this wonderful region. We welcome your comments and suggested additions. Please let me know what is "special" or "couple-friendly" about the recommendation.

I hope you enjoy this book as much as I enjoyed the research and the writing of it. Have a great time together,

Mandy Johnston

Although most of us feel we haven't enough time to spend together, there are a few places that seem to draw raves. If you have time to wander and browse, shop or buy, or are in the mood for some "edutainment," try one of the suggestions in this chapter. If this small sampling appeals, there are many more options along the same lines. Each of these locations has information about similar types of activities in the area. One simple date could lead to many days of leisurely explorations.

Chandler's Cove

901 Fairview Ave. N.
On Lake Union

Before, or after, a delicious meal at any of the nearby restaurants, you should explore Chandler's Cove. The little cluster of specialty shops is located right on the water, and offers everything from clothing to crystals to cookware. This can be an especially handy option while waiting for your table reservation, or for your name to come up at Cucina! Cucina! because they do not take reservations. It's also a pleasant way to end a romantic stroll along the lake. If you love sweets, stop in for a dessert or espresso at City Sweets, or pick up a picnic at the deli. A Versateller is also located in Chandler's Cove, just in case...

Chateau Sainte Michelle Winery

1411 NE 145th
Take Hwy 202 /2 miles south of Woodinville to 145th
Woodinville
488-1133 or 488-3300

Spending an afternoon at Chateau Sainte Michelle Winery makes a great date, no matter how long you have known each other. The winery has tours, which run every half hour, last about 45 minutes and are open to all ages (but you must be twenty-one to sample the wine). The tour is free.

The winery also presents popular outdoor concerts and other events in the Amphitheater. (Note: it is festival seating.) You can snuggle up on a blanket (bring your own) or you can bring folding chairs. Pack a romantic picnic, or buy one from Ste. Michelle (all alcoholic beverages must be purchased from the winery). During the holiday season carolling and other festive attractions take place indoors.

If you and your companion are athletic, you can ride bikes, or walk, to the winery via the Marymoor or Burke Gilman trails. Late fall is an especially pleasant time to visit, since the grapes are being pressed and the odor fills the air.

Chateau Sainte Michelle is open from 10:00 AM to 6:00 PM seven days a week. For tour information call 488-7733. More information on the Summer Festival can be obtained by calling 488-3300. For tickets to the Summer concerts, call Ticketmaster at 628-0888.

Ferry Boat Rides

Washington State Ferry System
464-6400 (information/schedules)

A trip on a Washington State Ferry can provide many pleasures. Take a picnic and enjoy the waterfront parks. Take bicycles, and explore the "island countryside." Boats leave from Seattle, Edmonds, Mukilteo and Fauntleroy. A nice trip is from Seattle to Bainbridge (formerly called Winslow). This little one-plus street town is easy to explore and has some interesting stops and shops. For dinner, the Saltwater Cafe (403 Madison) is right down on the waterfront marina. A popular breakfast spot is the Streamliner (397 Winslow East), which is on the main drag. Poulsbo is a quaint destination village about 12 miles away. It's a nice bike ride. Vashon Island (take the Fauntleroy ferry) also offers scenic bike touring, island shopping and good food options.

Gilman Village

317 NW Gilman Village Blvd.
Issaquah (I-90 exit #17, bear right)
462-0594

Gilman Village is a destination shopping "center" with a rustic theme. It's easy to spend the better part of a day exploring the various shops. All the stores in this cluster of buildings range from funky to boutique; this is *not* your average strip mall. Couples can be seen buying a balloon from the Red Balloon Company, a keepsake of dried flowers, a favorite book or shopping for gifts. The stores and restaurants in Gilman Village open at 10:00 on weekdays and Saturdays, 11:00 AM on Sundays, and close around 6:00 PM on weekdays and Saturdays, 5:00 PM on Sundays.

Here are three spots for pausing for a late lunch or snack, and a great little Italian restaurant, all within the boundaries of the Village:

The Feedstore (391-4671) is a quaint farm-like restaurant with an outdoor deck. You can enjoy salads and sandwiches to eat, and beer, wine and espresso to drink. The Feedstore accepts Visa, MasterCard and personal checks. The hours are 8:00 AM to 5:00 PM; during the summer they are open until 8:00 PM on Thursday nights. Entree prices: about $5.00.

The Art House Cafe (392-2648) is a funky bakery and gallery combination with outdoor and indoor seating. They serve Starbucks coffee and espresso treats. There is also a wide variety of baked goods, grilled European sandwiches and fresh blended yogurts. Art lovers will find this place an especially appealing late-afternoon snack spot. The Art House Cafe is open until 8:00 PM Thursday through Saturday, until 6:00 PM Monday through Wednesday, and until 4:00 PM on Sunday. Entree prices: about $5.00.

Nicolino Ristorante Italiano (391-8077) remains open later than the rest of Gilman Village. Dinner is served from 5:00 PM to 10:00 PM and seating is first come, first served. The decor is black and white checkered floors with small tables and marble tabletops, an Italian tenor on tape and an Italian fresco on the wall. There's also a small patio with tables around a fountain. The dress is casual. This authentic (the chef is from Italy) little restaurant is becoming very popular with Eastsiders. They are also open for lunch. The dress is casual and the meals are well priced. Nicolino Ristorante Italiano accepts Visa, MasterCard and personal checks. Entree prices: $8.00 to $12.00.

Japanese Garden and Tea Ceremony

Lake Washington Blvd. E.
North of E. Madison St.
Washington Park Arboretum
684-4725

After lunch, or a picnic in the Arboretum, a romantic stroll through the beautiful Japanese Garden can top off a wonderful afternoon together. The Japanese Garden recreates a compressed mini-scape of mountains, forests, lakes, tablelands and village. It is so peaceful and serene, you will find visiting it a very soothing experience. Wander through this enchanted garden, learning about the Japanese use of color, symbolism and tradition, or just enjoy the quiet beauty. You will encounter gold-fish ponds and the Tea House. Chado—The Way of Tea—is demonstrated on the third Sunday of each month, and is included with your admission fee. You can take part in this ancient Japanese ritual at 2:00 PM and 3:00 PM.

The Japanese Garden is open seven days a week, March 1 through November 30, from 10:00 AM (closing time varies with the season). The summer hours are from 10:00 AM to 8:00 PM and the garden is closed from December through February. Admission prices are as follows: General, nineteen to sixty-five, $2.00; Youth, six to eighteen and Seniors, (sixty-five and up), and Disabled persons, $1.00; children under five are free.

Museum of Flight

9404 E. Marginal Way S.
South Seattle
764-5720

For those intrigued by the world of flight, or just fascinated with learning new things, the Museum of Flight is a great destination. Explore the history of aviation, climb inside a cockpit and trace the steps to space exploration. Admission to the Museum of Flight is $5.00 for ages sixteen and over, $3.00 ages six to fifteen; children under six and museum members are free. The museum hours are from 10:00 AM to 5:00 PM daily and until 9:00 PM on Thursday.

After exploring the museum, find your way over to the east side of Boeing Field (7299 Airport Way South) and have a meal or a drink at the Blue Max Restaurant and Lounge. Located in the Passenger Terminal at Boeing King County Airport, the Blue Max is a great aviation fan's hangout. Both restaurant and lounge overlook the activity at Boeing Field. The funky bar atmosphere is a lot of fun (for couples over twenty-one years old), and features theme drinks and daily specials. There's dancing after 9:00 PM on Friday and Saturday, happy hour dollar busters, free hot food buffets, etc.

Just north of the terminal, The Aviator's Store is the perfect place to shop for a gift or souvenir related to the world of pilots and planes. The Aviator's Store (763-0666) is open from 9:00 AM to 6:00 PM Monday through Friday, from 9:00 AM to 5:00 PM on Saturday, and from 10:00 AM to 5:00 PM on Sunday.

Omnidome

Pier 59/Next to the Aquarium
Waterfront
622-1868

If you think bigger is better, the Omnidome is the place to take your date! Recent shows include *The Eruption of Mount St. Helen's: Then and Now, The Magic Egg: A Computer Odyssey* and *The Great Barrier Reef.* The giant 70mm film is projected onto a 180 degree curved dome screen, so that you feel as if you are part of the movie. Six speakers surround you with 1,200 watts of sound. You sit, well actually lay, side by side, in the center of all this excitement. The dress is very casual because you are practically lying on your back. The crowd ranges from six to sixty-plus, and every age seems to enjoy the shows.

The movies change, so you will want to call first to find out if the topic interests you and your partner. You will also need to call the Omnidome to find out the current showtimes. Shows run seven days a week, from 10:00 AM to 10:00 PM. The box office phone number is 622-1868. Prices for the Omnidome are: $5.95 for adults, $4.95 for children, and $3.95 for children under twelve.

The Pike Place Market

Upper level: First & Pike
Lower level: Western & Pike
Downtown Seattle/Waterfront

A trip to Seattle's Pike Place Market is a fun, and casual date for an early-morning, or all day outing. The stands themselves close down between 5:00 and 6:00 PM, but many of the restaurants are open later. The outdoor market includes fish stands and vendors offering fresh fruits and vegetables and various Northwest Arts and Crafts. If it's food you are looking for, the market has Turkish, Greek, Mexican and Oriental (to name only a few). For dessert, stop at one of the ice-cream or frozen yogurt shops, many of which also serve espresso.

People watching is perhaps one of the best things about the Market. Talking about the interesting people you see is one way to ease the awkwardness of a first-date. The Market is most lively during the warm, summer months, however the tourist crowds are larger as well. Off season, misty days have a whole different "Parisian" feeling and are more relaxed, if you don't like crowds. The various street and sidewalk musicians provide a touch of "culture" to your date; you'll hear everything from classical to folk, and lots in between.

A cash machine is located at the information booth, which is located in front of the fish market near the clock. On busy days, get your cash before you arrive; lines can be long or the machine can be emptied. How much money you spend is entirely up to where you go and what you eat or buy.

The Seattle Aquarium

1483 Alaskan Way/Pier 59
Waterfront
386-4320

Located on Pier 59, the Seattle Aquarium can be the perfect setting for an excursion. Anyone who loves the sea and marine life will find the aquarium fascinating. Wandering through the dark exhibits can even be romantic, and the location on Elliott Bay also makes the aquarium perfect for catching a sunset over the ferries and islands in Puget Sound. A rainy afternoon can be transformed into an underwater adventure, and on sunny days you can add a stroll along the busy waterfront area.

Aside from the "edutainment" of the exhibits and the marine life, the Seattle Aquarium is noted for sponsoring outdoor trips, special events, lectures and classes. Included among the many options are: kayak and canoe trips, cruises and field trips, snorkeling adventures and whale watching. There are also special opportunities for couples with kids.

You can become a member of the Aquarium Society, which entitles you to discounts on events sponsored by the Aquarium. (The public is invited to these events as well, at regular prices.) The Seattle Aquarium hours are: from 10:00 AM to 7:00 PM, Memorial Day to Labor Day, and from 10:00 AM to 5:00 PM, Labor Day to Memorial Day. The fees are: $6.00 for ages nineteen to sixty-four, $3.50 for ages six to eighteen, seniors and disabled, $1.00 for children three to five and free for children under two.

Waterfront Street Car

Pier 70 (Broad and Alaskan Way)
5th & Jackson/International District
553-3000 (Metro schedule and fare information)

Choose an alternative form of transportation for your day or evening activities and step back in time. The Waterfront Street car is an old fashioned trolley that runs all the way from Pier 70, at Broad Street, to the International District. It makes stops at the Pike Place Market, the waterfront piers and Pioneer Square, among others. There are dozens of eating and shopping options along the route.

The Street Car runs every day, but there are different hours for "winter" (September-February) and "summer" runs. Generally, the trolley operates from 7:00 AM until 6:00 PM, with additional runs during the summer until approximately 8:00 PM. Because the schedule varies, please call the Metro Info line before you make a date; they will also send you a current schedule of times and fares. Your ticket lets you ride for up to ninety minutes. The fares also vary according to season and time of day; generally plan on a maximum of $1.00 and a low of 75 cents. Compare these rates to cab fare from Pier 56 to Pioneer Square! Besides being economical, the trolley is a fun and different way to explore Seattle.

Westlake Center

1605 5th Avenue
Downtown Seattle
467-1600

Shopping can be a great way to spend time together, even if you are just window shopping. One of the more interesting places to shop is the Westlake Center in downtown Seattle. This place is like a museum for those who love the art of shopping! You will find more than eighty specialty stores, a food court and an outdoor plaza. You can try on fun clothes and hats, or check out the Northwest Tribal Art store or the Museum of Flight store. You can people watch or browse for books. If things get dull, you can take a ride on the Monorail (located just outside) to the Seattle Center.

The food court, called the Pacific Picnic, offers a variety of food options from hotdogs to Turkish specialties. Outside, when the weather is nice, you can listen to one of the numerous bands which perform in the plaza. Parking is available in the Westlake Center Parking Garage on Olive Way, between Fourth and Fifth Avenues.

The Westlake Center's hours change with the seasons. Winter hours: Monday through Friday 9:30 AM to 8:00 PM, Saturday 9:30 AM to 7:00 PM, and Sunday 11:00 AM to 6:00 PM. Summer hours: Monday through Friday 9:30 AM to 9:00 PM, Saturday 9:30 AM to 7:00 PM, and Sunday 11:00 AM to 6:00 PM. Winter hours last from December 27 to May 31 and summer hours are from June 1 to November 24. Shop 'til you drop!

Woodland Park Zoo

5500 Phinney Ave. N.
Phinney Ridge
684-4800

The Woodland Park Zoo is great fun for couples of all ages. If you haven't been to the zoo lately, you don't know what you are missing! Our zoo is considered one of the 10 best zoos in the country. A massive remodeling is in progress, which should be complete in 1997. The new gorilla and elephant exhibits are already finished and ready to view. The Tropical Rain Forest opened in September of 1992. If you want to take a picnic, there are tables available, or you can bring along a blanket. There are numerous snack bars with hot dogs, popcorn, cotton candy and all the great "zoo" favorites you loved as a kid. Sharing a cotton candy is a fine American romantic tradition!

Special events at the zoo include: Endangered Species Month in March, Conservation Day in June, Summer Concert Series in July and August and Wildlife Weekend in August. There are also many other events for zoo members only (if you'd like to join, give the zoo a call). The Summer Concert Series are quite popular, and are held in the zoo's North Meadow. Everything from folk to classical groups are headlined. Call to receive a complete schedule of groups and dates. The concerts begin at 7:00 PM., and you can top off a day at the zoo with an evening picnic and outdoor entertainment.

Admission is $5.00 for ages eighteen to sixty-four and $2.75 for ages six to seventeen, sixty-five and older, and disabled; children under five are free. The hours are 9:30 AM to 6:00 PM March 15-October 14, and 9:30 AM to 4:00 PM October 15-March 14. (The gates re-open for the Summer Concerts.) If you need more information call the zoo at 684-4800.

2 Exploring Cultural Attractions

Whether you are in the mood for a little culture or a lot of culture, you can choose from many opportunities in our area. Movies are included in this chapter because the theaters themselves vary greatly, from "arty" to "Hollywood," in both decor and films. All of the arts are represented, but not every location in the city is mentioned. The couples we sampled had their favorites, as will you.

ACT — A Contemporary Theater

100 W. Roy
Lower Queen Anne
285-5110

A Contemporary Theater—ACT—stages, you guessed it, contemporary plays. Generally, the plays focus upon the more recent playwrights. The mainstage season runs from May through November. However, in December ACT brings holiday audiences their very popular version of Dickens' *A Christmas Carol*. This traditional Christmas tale makes a wonderful December date for couples of all ages. ACT sometimes stages a winter production or two. The age range of the audience varies greatly, depending on the production, but is generally twenty-four to forty-plus. The ticket prices range from $12.00 to $24.00 and half price tickets are available at the ACT Box Office for "day of" productions. For information on the current plays and ticket prices, call the ACT box office at 285-5110.

Almost Live!

KING 5 Building
333 Dexter N.
Seattle
421-5555

A couple who loves to laugh, and loves the Pacific Northwest, will find *Almost Live!* a great dating idea. *Almost Live!* is a hilarious (local) late-night comedy show which airs right before *Saturday Night Live*. The show is taped at the KING 5 Television station in Seattle on weekend afternoons and evenings. The tickets are free and you must be at least sixteen years old. You can reserve up to four tickets, so make it a double date with your best friend. You will want to call first, find out what dates and times are available, reserve your space, then plan to be early because the seating is on a first come, first served basis. *Almost Live!* makes for a relaxed, fun, and free date. For more information and to reserve your tickets, call KING 5's *Almost Live!* line at 421-5555.

BDA (Bellevue Downtown Association)

500 !98th Avenue NE (Suite 210)
Koll Building/Downtown Bellevue
453-1223 (For information)

The Bellevue Downtown Association keeps Bellevue hopping with interesting, entertaining and cultural events. The noontime *On the Town* concerts are held in the various downtown plazas and run through July and August; if you both work in Bellevue, make a date for lunch and music. For Seniors, there are *Senior Tea Dances* held in Bellevue Square. These ballroom dances are held mid-afternoon, and are perfect for couples who love to dance. The BDA also brings us the *Pacific Northwest Arts and Craft Festival.* This (the most prestigious of its' kind in the northwest) multi-fair event takes place in and around Bellevue Square the last weekend in July and is an ideal date for art lovers. The *Taste of Bellevue* at the 6th Street Fair will take care of mealtimes between browsing through the stalls. *The Bellevue Jazz Festival* is held the second weekend in July, and takes place at Bellevue Community College. During the month of December, enjoy *Holiday Happenings;* these musical presentations take place in Bellevue Square and Bellevue Place. If you'd like to do a little "winter nibbling on the arts," consider the many events held during *Art Grazing* week. This celebration of the arts (culinary, visual and performing) is held the last week in January.

Belle Art Concerts

4800 139th Ave. SE
Lee Theatre
Ticket line: 454-2410

One of the eastside's most successful homegrown arts organizations is Belle Art Concerts, a chamber music series with a difference. For over a decade it has been the only chamber music series which presents regular programs to eastside audiences. Although local and regional artists are prominently featured in many concerts, the recent seasons have also included performances by celebrated musicians from throughout the world, such as the Shostakovich String Quartet from Russia.

As if fine music isn't enough, Belle Art offers its patrons ample free parking at the beautiful Lee Theatre high atop Somerset, an art exhibit, and an elegant complimentary post-concert buffet with an opportunity to meet internationally-acclaimed musicians.

Single ticket prices run $16.00 ($12.00 for students and seniors). Tickets are available by calling the Belle Art ticket line. All performances are held at 7:30 PM, and generally are held on Sunday evenings. It's a good idea to plan ahead since the concerts frequently sell out at least two weeks in advance.

Bellevue Art Museum

3rd Floor, Bellevue Square Mall
Downtown Bellevue
454-3322

BAM, as Eastsiders refer to it, may be located in a trendy shopping mall, but it is a serious museum, and a pleasant surprise. BAM's prime directive is "to advance the excellence of Northwest art and crafts through a program of exhibition, education and publication." The exhibits change frequently, and cover the subjects of architecture, crafts, drawing, painting, photography, sculpture, textiles. Traveling shows and exhibits sometimes range outside the northwestern arts community, or feature local artists with an international following. You can pick up an exhibition schedule, or call for details.

The museum hours are from 10:00 AM to 8:00 PM Monday and Tuesday, 10:00 AM to 6:00 PM Wednesday through Saturday and 11:00 AM to 5:00 PM Sunday. The gift shop is open from 9:30 AM to 9:30 PM Monday through Saturday. BAM gladly accepts your personal check. Admission fees are: $3.00 for adults, $2.00 for seniors and students, and BAM members are free. Every Tuesday is free admission for all ages (donations welcome). After the museum, try one of the mall restaurants for a nice dinner or a drink. Jungle Jim's and Jake O'Shaughnessey's are good options, and both have lively lounges in the evenings.

The Bellevue Repertory Theater

606 110th Avenue NE/Suite 211
Bellevue
454-5025

The Bellevue Repertory Theater is the first Equity professional theater group on the eastside, and began over ten years ago. The Rep stages a great Shakespeare in the Grass series at Bellevue Place and at Chateau Ste. Michelle. A new theater, home for the Company, is in the works in downtown Bellevue. Until the Meydenbauer Center Theater opens (1994), you can only enjoy the plays during summer months.

Cucina! Cucina! offers a great Box Supper deal for performances at Bellevue Place; you order your meal with your tickets. The food is not your ordinary picnic fare, and the prices are good. Beverages are available in the courtyard where the performances are held.

You can order tickets from the Bellevue Rep. Prices are from $8.00 to $10.00 and the dinners are form $5.00 to $8.00. Those who love Shakespeare, and who want to support this Equity theater company, will certainly enjoy these authentic, outdoor productions.

Elliott Bay Book Company
Elliott Bay Cafe

101 S. Main Street
Pioneer Square
Bookstore: 624-6600
Cafe: 682-6664

The Elliott Bay Book Company offers a unique way to spend "quality" time together. The bookstore itself is a fun place to explore. It's unlikely you won't find something you want to read among the thousands of titles (backlist and new) that fill the shelves to overflowing. If you can't locate that special book, they'll order it for you. The Elliott Bay Book Company is open from 10:00 AM to 11:00 PM, Monday through Saturday, and noon to 6:00 PM on Sundays.

Downstairs, there's a great little cafe. The tables are surrounded by tall bookshelves, accentuating the "intellectual" mood. Sandwich and soup type meals are available from about $2.50 to $5.00 each. Coffee, espresso and tea are also served for about $1.50, plus wines by the glass. The Cafe is open from 7:00 AM to 10:30 PM Monday through Friday, from 10:00 AM to 10:30 PM on Saturday, and from 11:00 to 5:30 PM on Sundays.

Besides visiting the bookstore and cozy cafe, you might consider attending one of the continuous string of readings by famous authors. All readings begin at 7:30 PM (unless otherwise specified) and a variety of subjects are represented. A monthly listing of the readings and discussions is available. For more information, call 624-6600, or stop by the store. The majority of the tickets are free, but a few special guest speakers require advance tickets (usually about $5.00). Well-known authors fill up early.

Fifth Avenue Theater

1308 5th Avenue
Downtown Seattle
625-1900

Impress your date with tickets to a musical at the Fifth Avenue Theater. This theater genre has made a strong come-back in Seattle, and the Fifth Avenue is largely responsible. The theater's architectural design recreates the throne room from ancient China's Forbidden City in Beijing. Surrounded by this magical setting, you will be treated to a wonderful production. A total of four shows are presented a year, some are locally produced and others are touring productions. The themes and shows cover the gamut of light opera and musical comedy. Nearly all the old favorites have been—or will be staged—plus at least one-per-season of the big hits from the current New York and London theatre scene.

The dress is typically on the dressy side, depending on what night and performance you choose to see. The subject matter determines the age of the audience. During intermission, you can refresh with coffee, sodas, pastries or a selection from the bar. There are restaurants within walking distance (see Duke's Fish House, the Palm Court and The Garden Court at the Olympic hotel under restaurants). Ticket prices range from $15.00 to $65.00, depending on the show and location of the seats, and are available through Ticketmaster (628-0888) or in person at the Fifth Avenue Box Office (Hours: 10:00 AM to 5:00 PM, weekdays only).

Frye Art Museum

704 Terry Street
Capitol Hill
622-9250

Add a touch of culture to your life, without spending a lot of money, at the Frye Art Museum. A few hours at the Frye combined with an espresso or glass of wine up on Broadway can be a great date. The museum is small (although there are 8 galleries in total) and has an intimate appeal. It was considered extremely advanced in gallery architecture of it's time (1952). The majority of the works are late Nineteenth Century, both European and American. In 1983, an Alaskan Wing was added for the specific display of Alaskan art.

The traveling shows change every month, and range from traditional to modern. The Watercolor Exhibit is especially noteworthy, as are other juried shows. You can pick up a newsletter free at the desk or add your name to their mailing list. The Museum is free of charge, which is a real bonus if you are on a tight budget. (Cash donations are accepted, and it's a nice way to support the arts.) The Frye Art Museum is open from 10:00 AM to 5:00 PM Monday through Saturday and from 12:00 PM to 5:00 PM Sundays.

Gallery Walk

The first Thursday gallery opening and walk is a cultural event, a see-and-be-seen opportunity and a sort of mini Mardi gras. Every first Thursday of every month, participating galleries from the Pike Place Market to the Kingdome—and especially in the Pioneer Square area—are open special hours from 6:00 PM to 8:00 PM. The adjacent bars, pubs and restaurants are also ready and waiting for couples ready to take a break. Art lovers and browsers from all over the Seattle area take advantage of these special hours and new openings. The dress is casual, although many people show up after work. However, if you and your date are coming straight from work, bring a comfortable pair of shoes.

If you are in a serious relationship, buying art together is a special experience. But besides viewing the art, this is a terrific people-watching event. Some of the more dramatically artistic outfits show up at the gallery openings! The age ranges from twenty to sixty-plus, and the crowd can get very large (even on rainy days). End the evening at one of the nearby drinking and dining establishments in Pioneer Square; there are many options, ranging from wild and funky to elegant and quiet or bohemian and artsy.

Henry Art Gallery

15th NE and NE 41st
University of Washington
543-2280

Located at the University of Washington, the small, but very interesting Henry Art Gallery focuses on contemporary art. Both international and national exhibits are featured. One thing about modern art, it always gives you something to talk about. You can call the museum ahead of time to see what is currently on display and how avant garde it might be. There is also a gallery bookstore and poster shop. General admission is $3.00, but University students and staff are free. Thursdays are also free admission to everyone. The museum hours are from 10:00 AM to 5:00 PM on Tuesday-Sunday, 10:00 AM to 9:00 PM on Thursday and closed on Monday. For more information call the museum at 543-2280.

Intiman Theater

201 Mercer Street
Seattle Center
Lower Queen Anne
626-0782

An intimate date, deserves an intimate play. Located on the Seattle Center grounds, the theater is small (426 seats) and has an intimate atmosphere. The productions focus on the actor and the spoken word; the plays themselves are intimate in their nature and deal with dialogue rather than action. They stimulate the intellect and give a couple a lot to discuss. The age range varies depending on the play, but college age and then thirty to fifty-plus make up the majority of the audiences.

The season runs from May to December. Ticket prices are regularly priced from $11.50 to $21.00 through Ticketmaster and the Intiman box office. However, there are other options. Ticket/Ticket sells them the day of the performance, for reduced prices. Students pay only $5.00 the day of the performance, and anyone can buy them at half price that day. The Intiman also has "pay what you can" performances. The minimum is $1.00 and these tickets sell fast, so call for more information on the dates of those shows.

Museum of History and Industry

2700 24th E.
Montlake area
324-1125 (recorded information) or 324-1126

A rainy day is the perfect opportunity to head for the Museum of History and Industry. Wandering through the permanent exhibits which trace Seattle's history and includes Northwestern history, you will learn many little-known facts about the city and the region. The main exhibits change about every three to five months, so you might want to call ahead and find out what is currently on display.

Admission prices are: General $3.00, children six to twelve, seniors and physically challenged $1.50, and under six free. On Tuesdays the admission is by donation only. The museum is open from 10:00 AM to 5:00 PM daily, and is closed Christmas, Thanksgiving and New Year's Day. They will accept your personal check.

The pleasant paths and trails along Lake Washington and into the Arboretum connect at the museum, so you can add a little natural history to your day. Bring walking shoes, and maybe an umbrella.

The Pacific Northwest Ballet (PNB)

Seattle Opera House/Mercer between 2nd and 4th
Lower Queen Anne
General Information: 547-5920 or 547-5900

The Seattle Opera House is home to our premiere ballet company, the Pacific Northwest Ballet. The season runs from October through June, and the Company presents twelve programs per year. Included in every season is "The Nutcracker." This Seattle tradition makes a wonderful holiday-time date. Anyone who loves beautiful music and the grace of ballet will enjoy dressing up for a special evening of dinner and a PNB performance. The age of the audiences varies, depending on the ballet and the show time. Tickets are available through the box office or through Ticketmaster. Ticket prices range from $10.00 to $50.00, depending on the seats, days and time of performance.

Seattle Art Museum

100 University
Downtown Seattle
654-3100

The "new" Seattle Art Museum is a great place to spend time together, especially if you both love art. The building is nearly as spectacular as the collections, and was the subject of considerable controversy during its construction. There are also state-of-the-art educational alcoves with videotapes, if you really want to get into the subject. (You can learn a lot about a person by finding out his/her tastes in art.) The exhibits change, so you will want to call and find out what is on display. There are also special activities like the authentic Tea Ceremony that are available by reservation only, plus other art+social happenings.

The museum is open from 11:00 AM to 5:00 PM Tuesday through Saturday, from 11:00 AM to 9:00 PM Thursday, and from noon to 5:00 PM on Sunday (closed Mondays). Admission is free every first Tuesday. Regular admission prices are $5.00 for adults and $3.00 for students and seniors. The Museum accepts all major credit cards and personal checks. The deli on the main floor serves sandwiches and salads for about $7.00 per person. Or you can just pause for a beverage break, and sip coffee, soft drinks, juices, beer or wine.

Seattle Opera

Mercer Street between 2nd and 4th
Lower Queen Anne
General Information: 547-5920 or 547-5900

A night at the opera is a classy date for all ages. The Seattle Opera series runs from August through May at the Opera House in the Seattle Center, and the following year's operas are announced in November. The English subtitles will help you understand exactly what is happening on stage. Founded in 1964, the Seattle Opera stages both traditional and contemporary works, plus the very popular Wagner's *The Ring* — which was first performed in Seattle in 1975.

The Opera House's architecture is beautiful, elegant and romantic. During the intermission, you can enjoy delicious desserts, soft drinks, wine and champagne or expressos. Evening performances begin at 7:30 PM and the Sunday performances begin at 2:00 PM. If you are planning dinner out pre-performance, you need to know that the opera starts promptly, so be on time. You can mail order single performance or season tickets from the Seattle Opera Office (389-7699), or you can buy individual performance tickets at the Ticket Office at the Opera House (389-7676).

Seattle Symphony

Opera House/Seattle Center
Offices: 4th floor/Seattle Center House
Ticket office: 443-4747

If music is the way to the heart of your loved one, why not surprise them with Seattle Symphony tickets? The Symphony usually calls the Opera House home, but they also hold special performances in other locations around the area (ie, the Chateau Ste. Michelle winery, the

Moore Theater, etc.). The season runs from September through June, with performances weekly. The concerts vary from classical to pop, with a special Discover Music series for couples with kids. Find out what composer, or instrument your companion likes in particular, then call the Seattle Symphony for suggestions. Make an evening of it, with dinner downtown first. Ticket prices vary. Depending on the performance and seats, expect to pay $9.00 to $65.00 per person. Tickets are available through the Seattle Symphony Ticket Office (443-4747).

Summer Nights at the Pier

Piers 62 and 63
Waterfront/Elliott Bay
441-6262

Summer nights are wonderful in and of themselves, but during July and August, they can be even more fun. Sponsored by Magnolia Hi-Fi and Cellular One, Summer Nights at the Pier is a concert series which take place on Piers 62 and 63 overlooking Elliott Bay. The setting is spectacular, the view of Puget Sound and West Seattle is incredible. The concerts are timed to catch sunset, which makes the setting even better. The series includes all kinds of music, from oldies to pop artists. The box office is located in front of the pier and the hours are from 11:00 AM to 6:00 PM, Tuesday through Sunday (closed on Monday). The ticket prices range from $16.00 to $22.00, depending on the show. (If you buy the tickets the same day of the show, add $2.00.) The ticket office phone number is 441-6262, for more information. You can pay with Visa, MasterCard, personal check or cash.

Ticket/Ticket

324-2744
401 Broadway East
Broadway Market (2nd level)
Validated parking in the Broadway Market Garage

1st & Pike
Pike Place Market Info. Booth
Validated parking in the Public Market Parking Garage

If your date includes seeing a show, but you are a little short of cash, go to Ticket/Ticket. With two convenient locations, Ticket/Ticket sells half-price tickets the day of the show,* for theater, music and dance events. These shows include tickets to The Backstage, Bathhouse, Broadway Performance Hall, Comedy Underground, Empty Space, Intiman, Jazz Alley, New City, New Image Theater, Pioneer Square Theater, Seattle Choral Co., Seattle Mime Theater, Seattle Opera and Seattle Symphony (to name a few). The ticket prices range from $3.75 to $15.00, sometimes a little more.

Ticket/Ticket is a walk-up service only, and accepts cash only. The hours are from 10:00 AM to 7:00 PM, Tuesday through Sunday at Broadway and from noon to 6:00 PM, Tuesday through Sunday at Pike Place. Ticket/Ticket makes it possible for everyone to see a good show, for a good price! They also sell coupon books, if you want to give that special someone a broad hint.

*Matinee tickets are sold the day before and day of, and Monday tickets are sold on Sunday.

University of Washington Arts Tickets Office
4001 University Way
University District
543-4880

The University of Washington stages a number of plays and musical and dance productions which offer a nice evening's entertainment. The UW also hosts a variety of touring groups. You can purchase tickets at the UW Arts ticket office, or at the theater on the night of the show. For information on what is playing and ticket prices, call the box office at 543-4880. The ticket office is open from 10:30 AM to 4:30 PM Monday through Friday.

You can also call the individual theaters: Meany Theater 685-2742, Glenn Hughes Playhouse 543-5646 and Penthouse 543-5638. The ticket prices range from a low of $5.00 for University presentations, to a high of $28 for headliners. Typically the age range of the audience is college age and from twenty-eight to thirty-something, but it varies greatly with the production.

Movie Theaters

Movies make great first dates and blind dates, because you don't have to talk for two hours. Then, when the movie is over, you have at least one thing to discuss. Movies also stimulate deeper discussions between good friends. Since the newspaper listings don't go much beyond the current screenings, here is some information about a selection of local theaters which range from the "far-out-funky" to "trendy-modern" in both the films that they show and the decor. The suggestions below are listed in alphabetical order.

Note: It's a standard among movie theaters to take cash only. No checks. No credit cards. The newer theaters have cash machines in the lobbies, but the best advice is to be sure you have a $20 bill in hand before you arrive.

Broadway Market Cinemas

425 Broadway E.
In the Broadway Market
323-0231

Catch the currently popular movies before or after you shop or eat and drink at the Broadway Market. The adult prices are $6.50; first show $4.00. (See page 80 for more information on the Broadway Market.)

Crest Cinema Center

16505 5th Avenue
Corner of NE 165th & 5th NE
Ridgecrest
363-6338

The Crest is a great cheap date spot, because all seats are $2.00, every day! There are also double-bill movies (where you can see two for one ticket) featured. There are five movie theaters. The Crest screens both "intellectual" fare and new, general-audience movies.

Crossroads Cinemas

1200 156th Ave NE
Behind the Crossroads Mall
Bellevue
562-7230

Crossroads is a newly remodeled cineplex which includes a total of eight theaters and shows the new, popular movies. Both exterior and interior are ultra-modern. There is a cash machine in the lobby, for your convenience. The theater is near numerous restaurants like Chili's, BurgerMaster, Black Angus and Ivars (to name a just a few). All shows before 6:00 PM are $3.50, and the regular adult price is $6.50.

Egyptian Theater

805 E. Pine
Capitol Hill
323-4978

The Egyptian is one large theater, reminiscent of the early days of movie-going. The films run from intellectual to current/popular, but lean toward the artistic. The latte stand right next door is handy for enjoying an espresso while you wait. Bill's Off Broadway is across the street, if you are in the mood for pizza. (See page 33 for more information on Bill's.) Adult ticket prices are $6.50. The community college parking lot across the street is only $2.00.

Factoria Cinemas

3505 128th SE
I-90 at 520/Bellevue
641-9206

With all the neon lights, you might wonder if you are at a theater or a space ride. Factoria features all current, popular films screened in eight theaters. There are also numerous video games in the lobby. The cineplex is across the street from The Keg restaurant and the popular Factoria Pub, and an assortment of chain and fast food places are close by as well. Adult ticket price is $6.50, and all shows before 6:00 PM are $3.50.

Grand Illusion Cinema

1403 and 1405 NE 50th
University District
523-3935

The Grand Illusion is Seattle's last independent and locally operated moviehouse. It screens off-beat/alternative films for fairly short runs. Ticket prices are $6.00 ($3.00 for kids and seniors) and the matinee prices are $4.00. (See page 101 for information about the Grand Illusion Cafe.)

Guild 45th Theatres

2115 N. 45th
Wallingford
633-3353

The Guild 45th features intellectual films. Both theaters are old and comfortable in a funky sort of way. Located across the street from the Beeliner Diner, next to My Brothers Pizza and a few doors from Goldies Tavern, it's easy to make a night of it. On the corner of 45th and Meridian there is a great "pub and grub" bar called Murphy's, which often features live music on weekend nights. Adult price at the Guild 45th is $6.50 and the first show is $4.00.

Harvard Exit Theatre

807 Harvard
Capitol Hill
323-8986

It's worth arriving early for the show just to spend time in the huge foyer of the Harvard Exit. Built and occupied by a suffragist group known as The Women's Century Club, this building reeks of times long gone. Besides the "living room" with it's ancient rug, creaky floor, chess tables, sofas and fireplace (and resident ghost), there are two large theaters. The Harvard Exit screens currently popular, intellectual and foreign films. Prices are $6.50 for adults; $4.00 for the first show. The Harvard Espresso is across the street, and of course there are dozens of after-movie options nearby on Broadway.

Kirkland Parkplace Cineplex

3505 128th SE
Downtown Kirkland: Parkplace Center
827-9000

The Parkplace Cineplex features current and popular movies. It is located right below T.G.I. Fridays, so you can make it dinner and a movie without moving your car. There are a total of six movie theaters from which to choose. While you wait, you can walk around the mall, or sit by the fountain and talk. The adult price is $6.50 and all shows before 6:00 PM are $3.50.

Metro Cinemas

4500 9th Street
In the Metro Center
University District
633-0055

The Metro Cinema has ten theaters and screens both popular and intellectual films. The theaters are very modern and comfortable. Stella's is located on the first floor; this Italian restaurant is open twenty-four hours a day, which is very convenient if you want to talk all night. The Keg restaurant is on the other side of the building on Roosevelt Avenue, if you are in the mood for non-Italian selections or a salad bar. Adult price $6.50 and first shows are $4.00.

Neptune Theater

1303 NE 45th
University District
633-5545

The Neptune Theater is located right near the "Ave" in the U District, so your choice of nearby pubs, tavs and restaurants is numerous. You can also always find a late-night coffee shop to enjoy a late-night dessert or espresso. This funky old theater features intellectual and artsy films. Across the street from the theater there is a bank with a Readyteller. The adult price is $6.00 and first shows are $4.00. There are also late night shows on Friday nights.

Seven Gables Theatre

911 NE 50th
University District
632-8820

Built in what looks like an old house, the Seven Gables Theater features intellectual films. There is only one theater, and it is small and comfortably worn. The adult price is $6.50 and the first show is $4.00. The Seven Gables Theater is close enough to the University District that you can eat first and be at the theater within minutes. The popular Italian restaurant, Mama Molina's, is just a few doors down on Roosevelt.

Uptown Cinemas

511 Queen Anne Ave. N.
Lower Queen Anne
285-1022

The Uptown has three theaters which screen popular movies. The complex is fairly modern. The theater is next to Kidd Valley and across from Dick's hamburgers. Lower Queen Anne has a full range of dining and drinking options within walking distance (Ristorante Pony, Queen Anne Bar and Grill, Chicagos, Jake O'Shaunessey's, Duke's, Vince's, Pizzeria Pagliacci, for a short list). The Seattle Center is nearby as well. The adult price is $6.50 and the bargain matinee is $3.50.

Varsity Theater

4329 University Way NE
University District
632-3131

The Varsity features mostly intellectual films, but you can also catch the popular shows. There are three theaters, so you can usually find something you will both like. Located right on the University of Washington "Ave," you will see all sorts of interesting people inside and outside of the theater. Restaurants, bars and coffee shops are plentiful along the Ave, and in the general vicinity. The adult price is $6.50 and all shows before 6:00 PM are $4.00.

It wouldn't be hard to eat out every single night in and around Seattle and never exhaust the possibilities. The couple-tested places in this chapter run from the ultra-casual (a drive-in), to after-work havens, to quiet corners where you can retreat from the world for a meal without making a big deal of it. Generally, these are casual places for sharing a meal between friends, new-found or old. You can choose from a variety of cuisines and a full range of dining hours. For seriously romantic dining, see Chapter 3, and for places that cater to an all-evening or lively-lounge mood, see Chapter 4.

Beeliner Diner

2114 N. 45th
Wallingford
547-6313

The Beeliner is one of a kind. This funky spot is a great choice for breakfast, lunch or dinner. The atmosphere is friendly and relaxed. The waitress calls you "honey" and the cooks all have something to say. You can sit at the counter and watch your meal prepared, or sit at a booth. There is some music, but the majority of the noise comes from conversation and kitchen sounds. The age ranges from twenty-five to forty on the weekends, and from thirty to forty-five during the week. However, teens are not an uncommon sight.

The Beeliner is not the place for a romantic dinner, but it is a fun place for a casual meal *a deux*. The Guild 45th Theater is right across the street, and several notable pubs are within walking distance (Goldies and Murphy's to name the two closest ones). The menu includes American standards like hot dogs, steak and salad, and "modern American" and vegetarian entrees like stuffed black bean chillies with Anaheim cheese, nut burgers and eggplant with pesto; everyone should be able to find something appealing.

The Beeliner's hours are: Monday through Thursday 9:00 AM to 10:00 PM, Friday and Saturday 9:00 AM to 11:00 PM and Sunday 9:00 AM to 10:00 PM. They don't take reservations, but they do take all major credit cards and personal checks. Entree Prices: $3.25 to $9.75.

Bill's Off Broadway

725 East Pine Street
Capitol Hill
323-7200

A pizza place for true pizza lovers, Bill's Off Broadway serves up some of the best pizza in town. A variety of "classic" pasta entrees are also available. The interior is rustic, with rough-hewn wood walls and wooden tables and chairs. The atmosphere is definitely casual. You can watch the pizzas being made as you walk in the door. Bill's serves every pizza under the sun, from plain cheese to The Big 13 (you guessed it, thirteen toppings). A television set brings you big sporting events, and there is a small adjoining bar. The typical age range is from twenty to forty-plus.

Bill's is a good spot for a casual evening out. The Egyptian theater is right across the street (see page 27) and Bill's is open late, if you have an after-the-movie-pizza-attack. Hours are: Monday through Thursday 11:00 AM to 12:00 AM, Friday 11:00 AM to 1:00 AM, Saturday 12:00 AM to 1:00 AM, and Sunday 12:00 PM to 12:00 AM. Bill's accepts Visa, MasterCard and personal checks, and validates parking in the Seattle Community College Garage right across the street. No reservations necessary. Pizza prices: $6.50 to $20.00; entree prices: $4.50 to $7.75.

Burgermaster Drive-ins

10606 NE Northup Way
Bellevue/Kirkland border
827-9566

9820 Aurora Avenue N.
North Seattle
522-2044

A drive-in restaurant like Burgermaster can be either romantic or casual, but it's definitely a date from the past history of romance in our country. These locations are the only Burgermasters with car service—a legendary dating ritual for couples from the 30s to the 60s. The romantic appeal comes from having your own private dining room (your car) and your favorite tape playing in the background (in the "old days," it was your radio, of course). But it's also casual because you are eating burgers and fries in your car. Whichever type of arrangement you select, Burgermaster will provide an inexpensive and delicious dinner served on a window tray hooked to the side of your car. Big, juicy burgers can be special ordered with all the condiments you like (watch those onions!).

The service stalls are filled with cars whose occupants range from sixteen to sixty-plus. Sixteen year-olds will enjoy showing off their new car, and sixty year-olds will feel sixteen again. Burgermaster is open from 7:00 to 2:00 AM, Monday through Friday, and from 10:00 to 2:00 AM Saturday and Sunday. The late night hours make Burgermaster a great place to go after a movie. Dinner costs about $5.00 per person.

Note: Other Burgermasters (without the drive-in feature) are located in:

Bothell: 8002 NE Bothell Way (485-343)
Lynnwood: 18411 Hiway 99 (774-5831)
Bellevue: 1350 156th NE (522-2939)

Chandler's Crabhouse and Fresh Fish Market

901 Fairview Avenue N.
Southeast Lake Union
223-2722

Located on Lake Union, Chandler's Crabhouse is designed much like the Farmer's Market in The Pike Place market. The casual atmosphere and view of the lake and boats makes it a great choice for an evening of good food and casual conversation. The restaurant can get noisy, not with music, but with the sounds of conversation. The dress varies from casual to work attire, and the general look is "casually relaxed." As expected, Chandler's is famous for seafood. The menu changes regularly, and includes "Guaranteed Signature Items," which are guaranteed to please or are "on the house."

The crowd is a variety of ages, but is mainly composed of the early to mid-thirties. Chandler's is proud to have been voted by the Bite of Seattle '92 to have "Seattle's Best Crab Cakes." Look for them on the menu, both as a starter, and as an entree.

The bar serves mostly as an after work spot, and is almost part of the restaurant. Dinner is served every night until 11:00 PM. The bar closes, "when everyone leaves!" Smoking tables are available upon request. Entree prices: $15.00 to $35.00. Reservations are strongly suggested for weekend nights, and free parking is available in the Chandler Cove parking garage.

Cousins

140 Central Way
Kirkland
822-1076

Dinner is not the only meal you and your special someone can enjoy together. Why not try breakfast? Going out to breakfast is an ideal way for two busy people to make a date, and Cousins serves one of the best breakfasts in the area.* The atmosphere is warm and friendly. The noise level is moderate to loud; there's lots of conversation going on, and the surfaces are hard. The tables are fairly close together, so don't expect privacy.

Cousins serves big, delicious breakfasts, fresh fruits, and espresso. They don't take reservations, so it is first come, first served. On weekends, the earlier you get there, and get your name on the list, the sooner you will eat! Located in downtown Kirkland, you can take a nice

STEPPING OUT IN SEATTLE

walk along the trendy main street or beside Lake Washington to burn off some of the calories. Breakfast at Cousins runs $6.00 to $10.00.

For additional breakfast ideas, see Bibliography, page 131.

Ivar's Acres of Clams Restaurant and Seafood Bar

Pier 54
Waterfront
624-6852

Located right on the water, the Fish Bar makes for a fun, casual date for the fish and chip loving couple. It's also a good place for clams and chips and oysters and chips lovers. You can sit out on the deck, watch the ferries ply the Sound, and feed the seagulls. Perfect for warm summer nights. The dress is as casual as you want to make it. This spot is inexpensive, and stays open until 2:00 AM daily and year-round, so a late dinner is always available. Meals are about $5.00 per person. They accept Visa, Mastercard and personal checks. However, after 11:00 PM, it is cash only please.

Around the corner you'll find Ivar's Acres of Clams. This indoor restaurant and lounge is a little dressier and attracts an older crowd. Typically, the age range is twenty-five and older, but during the tourist season you'll find all ages. The atmosphere is casual and relaxed. The dress is casual to nice (no cutoffs, etc.). The lounge serves appetizers and is more a place to wait for a table then a hopping bar. Ivar's has long been known to serve a great, fresh seafood dinner. There are a few non-marine selections like beef and chicken entrees. The restaurant is open from 11:00 AM to 11:00 PM, every night during the summer; winter hours are 11:00 AM to 10:00 PM on weeknights. All major credit cards and checks are accepted. Entree prices: $15.00 to $20.00.

Ivar's Salmon House and Fish Bar

401 NE Northlake Way
Wallingford/on Lake Union
632-0767

Ivar's Salmon House and Fish Bar is the location of both a nice restaurant and a fast food bar. This makes it ideal for any kind of date. The inside of the Salmon House is modeled on a Northwest Indian theme, with totem poles and a hand carved canoe. The house specialty is alder smoked entrees prepared on the open firepit. The Seattle Weekly voted theirs the "best salmon in Seattle."

With a beautiful, close up, view of Lake Union, the restaurant attracts a sophisticated and mellow crowd. Happy hour in the lounge is on Friday from 4:00 to 6:30 PM, and things can get fairly loud. However, after that time a couple can relax and enjoy a peaceful drink. The typical age range of the crowd is forty and over. The dress is casual to nice and business attire is a very common sight at dinner. The dining room serves dinner from 4:30 to 11:00 PM Monday through Friday, from 4:00 to 11:00 PM on Saturday and from 4:00 to 10:00 PM on Sunday. The Salmon House accepts Visa, Mastercard and personal checks. Entree prices: $15.00 to $20.00.

The Fish Bar serves from 11:00 AM to 10:00 PM Sunday through Thursday, and 11:00 AM to 11:00 PM Friday and Saturday (until midnight on weekends in the summer). You can take your food around to the waterfront deck, or have a picnic at nearby Gas Works Park. The Fish Bar prices are $5.00 to $7.00 per person. Sitting out on the deck at night, under the stars, can make for a romantic (and inexpensive) late date.

Kamon on Lake Union

1171 Fairview Avenue N.
West Lake Union
622-4665

Kamon at Lake Union is really three restaurants in one. There is a sushi bar, the Pacific Rim dining room and a Teppan dinning room. The sushi bar is ideal for a casual date, if you enjoy this delicacy; you can sit right at the bar to observe the preparation, or do without watching and sit at tables. If sushi isn't your thing, try the Pacific Rim, which serves an international cuisine. Northwest favorites are included on the menu in this section of the restaurant. In the Teppan dining room, your food is cooked right in front of you, like Benihana of Tokyo (which is owned by the same company).

Obviously, Kamon has something to fit any occasion. There is even a Piano Bar with live music every Thursday through Saturday, from 7:30 to 11:30 PM. The restaurant is elegant Oriental design and the dress tends to run from casual to dressy. The sushi bar is much more casual then the other two dining rooms. The typical age range is from mid-twenties to late thirties—the very crowd that we have to thank for the popularization of sushi. There is a nice view of Lake Union, and you can eat outside on the deck during the summer.

Dinner is served from 5:00 PM to 10:00 PM Sunday through Thursday, and from 5:00 PM to 11:00 PM Friday and Saturday. Kamon does take reservations and accepts Visa, Mastercard and American Express. Entree Prices: $15.00 to $30.00.

Kidd Valley

5910 Lake Washington Blvd. NE
Kirkland
827-5888

Don't rule out Kidd Valley just because it is fast food! This is "fast" food prepared fresh daily on the premises and cooked while you watch. Kidd Valley was rated the Best Cheeseburger and a Favorite Place for Burgers by Eastside Week, 1992. The Kirkland restaurant is very new and fresh-looking, and the service is fast. You can eat outside and watch the sunset over Lake Washington. Another great idea is to take your order to one of the many Kirkland beaches for a picnic. (Marsh park is only a half a block down the street.) Kidd Valley in Kirkland is open from 10:30 AM to 9:00 PM Monday through Saturday, and from 11:00 AM to 9:00 PM on Sunday. The price range is about $5.00 per person.

For those of you old enough, or native-Northwestern enough to remember, Herfy's and Kidd Valley and Dick's were the original local burger chains. Now Ivar's owns Kidd Valley, but after all, they're a home-grown chain as well. Other Kidd Valleys (without views) are located at:
6434 Bothell Way NE, Bothell (485-5514)
4910 Greenlake Way N., Seattle (547-0121)
15259 Bel-Red Road, Bellevue (643-4165)

La Cocina del Puerco

10246 Main Street
Old Bellevue
455-1151

Truly authentic Mexican food is unusual in the northwest, but you can find it at La Cocina Del Puerco, located in Old Bellevue. Don't expect the usual nachos and burritos, however.

The food is served cafeteria style, and is very mild, unless you load on the hot salsas and jalapeños. The atmosphere is funky, cantina-Mexican, with piñatas and Mexican signs hung from ceiling and walls, and authentic metal tables and chairs. There are tables outside, much like the outdoor tables in Mexico and Spain. Inside, the tables are fairly close together; although it isn't very private, it's a companiable mood. The music is Mexican, and can be loud—add a full house and it's not a quiet ambiance. In warm weather, you can sit outside and watch the foot and automobile traffic on Main Street, while enjoying a cool drink and hot dinner. The dress is as casual as the surroundings, and the age range is typically from twenty-five to fifty-plus.

La Cocina Del Puerco is open from 11:30 AM to 9:00 PM, Monday through Thursday, from 11:30 AM to 10:00 PM, Friday and Saturday and from 1:00 PM to 9:00 PM on Sunday. No reservations are taken, and on busy nights you'll search for a table. They accept major credit cards, but no personal checks. Entree prices: $4.00 to $7.50.

Mama's Mexican Kitchen

2234 Second Ave (at Bell St.)
Downtown/Belltown area
728-6262

Mama's Mexican Kitchen serves Southern California-Style Mexican Food, and looks like a Southern California/Baja hole-in-the-wall. Nevermind the very casual ambiance, the food is great! This place was possibly the first Mexican restaurant in the area (opened in 1974*), and it's been going strong ever since. The interior looks like it belongs in Los Angeles somewhere, with it's vinyl booths and bright news flyers on the walls. Outdoor seating is available during the summer, right out on the downtown city sidewalk. Mama's is loud and busy, like any good Mexican restaurant should be, and the beer is cold.

All of the Mexican-American favorites are on the menu, and there's even a *not hot* item called "Screamers." Mama's Mexican Kitchen was rated one of the best Ethnic Restaurants in Seattle and you will see why. If you and your companion want to experience something a little different in the way of dining out, try Mama's. Plan on having a great time, but don't plan on dressing up. Entree prices: $3.50 to $8.75. Personal checks and credit cards are welcome.

*The first Mama's started in Hawaii, and there are now 3 locations in the Islands. All, including the Seattle restaurant, are still operated by the same owner.

Mamounia Moroccan Restaurant

1556 East Olive Way
Captitol Hill
329-3886

Couples who enjoy trying new foods will love Mamounia. The decor recreates the interior of a nomadic tent—like something out of the Arabian Nights. The walls are covered with patterned drapes and the waiters wear traditional Moroccan dress. You sit on the floor on low cushions, or on pillow covered benches which line the "tent." Despite the exotic, intimate surroundings, the tables are so close together that there is not a lot of privacy. In keeping with the customs of Morocco, you eat all the food with your hands. (You might want to warn your date about this fact.) However, you can order wine or beer—a departure from the cultural norms.

The meal is served in various courses, and begins with the waiters washing your hands. Then the courses arrive one by one, for you to enjoy in a leisurely fashion. Mamounia serves dinner from 5:00 PM to 10:00 PM Tuesday trough Sunday; closed Mondays. They accept credit cards, but no personal checks. The fixed price six course dinners are either $16.50 or $18.50, depending upon your choice of main entree.

Maximilien in the Market

81A Pike Street
Pike Place Market (look to the left, under the clock)
682-7270

Maximilien French Cafe ("*un restaurant-cafe tres Francais*") looks like you just jet-setted over to France for dinner. The all-wood atmosphere is distinctly French, with wine bottles decorating the walls. But the view of Elliot Bay reminds you that you are still in Seattle, Washington. The menu is, you guessed it, French! The dinner menu changes nightly and includes fresh fish items, beef, lamb, veal and other continental entrees. Monday through Thursday a four course meal, including soup, salad, an entree and dessert, is available. The price of the four course meal ranges from $13.00 to $18.00. Although the food is French, many of the courses are on the "light" side.

Typically, the crowd tends to be early thirties and up, however those in their twenties will also enjoy this spot. The dress can range from casual to extremely dressy. Casual Market-goers are as common as pre-opera customers in Maxmilliens. The air of romance is everywhere, much like Paris, and Maximiliens makes an ideal "special occasion" choice. Maximiliens accepts all major credit cards, but no personal checks. Dinner is served Monday through Saturday, 5:30 until 10:00 PM, and reservations are recommended. Brunch (menu selections) is served on Sunday from 9:30 to 4:00 PM. Entree prices: $15.00 to $25.00.

Metropolitan Grill

818 2nd Avenue
Downtown Seattle
624-3287

The Metropolitan Grill claims to serve the best steak in town, and Seattleites seem to agree. The restaurant is designed to resemble a restaurant in Manhattan, or any other similarly urban and urbane setting. The booths are steeped in deep, green velvet and brass. The noise level is medium to loud; this is a place where people talk a lot over their meals. The age range is mostly early thirties and up, thanks to being the perfect location for the city's "after work" crowd. There is a bar which closes with the restaurant, and is most definitely an after work watering hole. The dress is "professional." It is not uncommon for people to be dressed up and en route to the theater.

The menu includes seafood, pasta, chicken and steak—"Seattle's Award Winning" variety—and excellent prime rib. The Chateubriand for Two deserves a special note, and is carved right at your table. Dinner is served from 5:00 to 11:00 PM Monday through Saturday, and until 10:00 PM on Sundays (also open for brunch when the Seahawks play). Reservations are strongly suggested. There is on-street parking, or in the parking garage across the street. The Metropolitan Grill accepts all major credit cards, and personal checks with proper identification. Entree prices: $15.00 to $20.00.

Morgan's Lake Place Bistro

2 Lake Bellevue Drive
Off Bel-Red Road at 120th St.
455-2244

Morgan's Lake Place Bistro sits on Lake Bellevue, Bellevue's only urban lake (sometimes called "fake lake," although the water and the ducks are quite real). Outdoor seating is available during the warmer months, and you are right on the water. During the day, you can watch the ducks and geese paddling about on the lake. Inside, the atmosphere is casual and almost rustic. You and your companion will enjoy a relaxed and comfortable dinner.

Morgan's is one of the most successful Eastside restaurants; their formula is high quality, well-priced food (pastas, seafood, poultry, beef, salads, appetizers) and great service in a pleasant decor. The music is soft and the lights are dim. The typical age range is from about thirty to fifty-plus, although everyone in between is seen and welcome (including kids). The dress is casual to nice.

Dinner is served from 5:30 to 9:00 PM Sunday through Saturday and until 10:00 PM on Friday nights, and the bar is open until 1:00 AM. The lounge has its followers, mostly from the professional crowd. Reservations are suggested and Morgan's accepts major credit cards. Entree prices: $10.00 to $20.00.

Northlake Tavern

660 NE Northlake Way
University District/Lake Union
633-5317 ("to go" phone)

The Northlake Tavern serves Seattle's heftiest pizza and provides a fun and lively atmosphere for a casual dinner date. The brightly painted walls show cartoons displaying U.W. characters and pizza jokes. (Note: The Northlake Tavern *is* a tavern, and a valid ID is required.) The typical age range is from twenty-one to sixty+, with the majority current or past students at the U.W. or boaters from the nearby marinas. Be prepared for a loud and always crowded dining experience. The tables and booths are fairly close together, so there isn't a lot of privacy, but the Northlake provides a casual and relaxed atmosphere, plus that legendary pizza that has kept lines forming since 1952. Be prepared to put your name on the list, and wait up to 45+ minutes, especially on weekend nights. "Take-out" pizza is yet another option, but you need to call first!

The Northlake's hours are from 1:00 to 11:00 PM on Sunday, from 11:00 PM to 12:00 AM on Monday through Thursday, and from 11:00 PM to 1:00 AM on Friday and Saturday. The pizza price depends on what you put on it, but generally from $10.00 to $20.00 per pizza. There are "classic Italian" entrees as well, but most everyone comes for the pizza. The Northlake Tavern accepts Visa and Mastercard, but no personal checks.

The Pink Door

1919 Post Alley
Pike Place Market
443-3241

This Italian restaurant can only be found by, you guessed it, it's pink door. Located on Post Alley, the Pink Door has no sign, just that pink door as its well-known landmark. Inside, the European setting is charming. The atmosphere is romantic, continental style, with candles on the floral tablecloths and out on the deck as well. The Pink Door serves a four course Italian dinner which changes weekly. This four course meal, and the manner in which it is served, makes for an impressive date.

The Pink Door brings in all age groups, but the majority are twenty five and over. During the warmer months, sitting out on the deck, under the stars, makes for an incredibly romantic night. Reservations are a must, especially if you want to sit outside. Dinner begins at 5:30 and the last serving is at 10:00 PM. Smoking is only allowed outside on the deck. Dinner price: $17.50 for a four course meal served in the dining room; the bar service is á la carte (price range $6.50-$8.50). Lunch is about the same as the bar prices. The Pink Door accepts major credit cards and cash only.

The Poor Italian Cafe

2000 2nd Avenue at Virginia
Downtown Seattle
441-4313

The Poor Italian Cafe's motto is "You'll feel rich with the taste of Italy." But you don't have to be rich to enjoy this restaurant. The cafe looks like it might sit on a street in Italy, with tile floors, brick walls and white linen tablecloths. At night, when the lights go down, the restaurant can be very romantic. Quiet, Italian music can be heard playing softly in the background. The Poor Italian is an ideal date spot because of it's a pleasant ambiance and the prices are reasonable. The dress ranges from casual to very dressy, and everything in between.

Its downtown location makes the Poor Italian a nice "pre-theater" spot. The crowd tends to be a combination of the after-work group and a little younger. The average age is twenty-one to thirty-five. There is a small, adjoining bar, which is fairly quiet and mostly used by customers waiting for a table. Dinner is served from 4:00 PM to 10:00

PM Monday through Thursday, from 4:00 PM to 11:00 PM Friday and Saturday, and from 4:30 PM to 9:00 PM on Sunday. Smoking is available in designated areas only. Reservations are suggested, if you don't want to wait for a table. Entree prices: $8.00 to $10.00. All major credit cards and personal checks are accepted.

Stella's Trattoria

4500 9th NE
University District
633-1100

Stella's Trattoria is a warm and friendly restaurant with good Italian food. Open 24 hours a day, it's also an ideal late night spot (See page 105). You can see a movie at the Metro cineplex upstairs, then come down to Stella's for a midnight snack. The dinner menu is served from 4:00 PM until 11:00 PM, then a late night menu is served, which is a mix of dinner and breakfast options. The atmosphere is casual and very comfortable. The walls are covered with art and posters, and there are plants all around. The little wood tables and high walls give Stella's the feeling of an outdoor cafe. The age ranges from twenty-one to fifty-plus, depending on the hour. Stella's accepts all major credit cards and personal checks. Entree prices: $5.50 to $12.50.

4 Setting the Stage for Romance

When you are ready to pull out all the stops, dress up instead of down, share a divine meal and let cupid do his thing, you'll be safe selecting from the following restaurants. Some of these restaurants are very reasonable, some are pricey, and not all require best attire. Whether it's time to move into a more serious relationship, finalize love with a proposal of marriage, or just renew the many good times you've shared together, these places are deliberately focused on providing the right ambiance.

Adriatica Restaurant

1107 Dexter N.
Queen Anne
285-5000

Big picture windows look out over Lake Union. Thanks to being a remodeled home, there are several small, cozy dining areas. The understated interior means that you focus on each other and the view and the food. White linen tablecloths and little table lamps, soft background music, outstanding service, and excellent food make this one of the most popular restaurants with couples in search of a special evening out. Adriatica opened in 1977, and has received various awards ("Best Ethnic," and "Best of the Northwest" among them).

The mood runs from casual to romantic, but the dress is generally on the professional to dressy side. Dinner is served seven nights a week, from 5:30 PM to 10:00 PM from Sunday through Thursday, and from 5:30 to 11:00 PM on Friday and Saturday. Reservations are strongly suggested. Adriatica accepts major credit cards and personal checks, with proper identification. Entree prices: $13.50 to $19.50.

The bar is located upstairs, and serves appetizers. Bar hours are 5:00 PM to 1:00 PM, nightly. This is an ideal late-night option after a movie or an event at The Seattle Center.

Cafe Sophie

1921 First Avenue
Downtown Seattle
441-6139

Charming is the first word which comes to mind when describing this restaurant decorated in dark green draperies. Private little alcoves are available for your intimate dates. Each table has a little light that mimics candlelight. Outdoor seating is available, weather permitting, on the sidewalk patio. The crowd varies, as does the dress. During "prom season," this restaurant is popular with young couples in formal wear. However, the casually dressed couple will not feel out of place and there is no dress code. Generally speaking, the patrons are a little older due to the price and sophisticated atmosphere. The nouveau cuisine includes a variety of entrees, including chicken, fish, pasta and salads (to name a few).

Dinner is served from 5:00 PM to 10:00 PM Sunday through Thursday, and from 5:00 PM to 11:00 PM Friday and Saturday.

Reservations are strongly suggested on weekend nights. Cafe Sophie gladly accepts local personal checks, Visa and MasterCard. Entree prices: $11:00 to $30.00.

Campagne

86 Pine Street
Pike Place Market
728-2800

Campagne serves French country-style cuisine and is a totally enchanting restaurant. It is romantic enough to celebrate a special occasion, and quaint enough for a cozy get-to-know each other. The outdoor Courtyard dining area sits in the middle of the brick and ivy building. A quiet fountain gives the Courtyard an extra touch of romance. Indoors, the decor is wood and linen and *très* French. The dress tends towards dressy; sometimes tourists are more casual than local couples on a special night out. The noise and music level is quiet enough to allow for an intimate conversation. The food is Provincial French, and the menu varies so that everyone can find something to suit his/her taste.

Dinner is served from 5:30 to 10:00 PM and the Courtyard and bar are open until midnight. A "late night" menu is offered in both the Courtyard and bar. Reservations are a must on weekend nights. The typical age range is thirty and over, although anyone in their twenties or fifties will love this place. Campagne accepts all credit cards, but no personal checks. Entree prices: $16.00 to $24.00.

Eques

900 Bellevue Way NE
In the Hyatt Regency Hotel
Downtown Bellevue
462-1234

Tucked away inside the Hyatt Regency Hotel, Eques provides a romantic and elegant, old-world setting. The tables are well spaced (and beautifully draped), to allow for private conversations. The lights are dim, and the music is unobtrusive and soothing. The typical age range is thirty-five to forty-five, with the exception of senior proms. The clientele appears well-to-do, as befits the restaurant's atmosphere, but Eques is a great place to enjoy a nice, but not bankrupting dinner.

The dress is usually dressy, with a few in casual-nice outfits. The service is always friendly, and the food is very good. The giant scallops and prawns are favorites of many customers. Reservations are suggested. Eques accepts major credit cards. Valet parking is available (validated with your meal) at the Hyatt, and there is also validated self-park underneath the hotel complex. Eques serves from 6:30 AM to 10:30 PM, seven days a week. Entree prices: $10.95 to $18.95.

Eques has a very appealing lounge area adjacent to the restaurant. As contrasted to the soft tones of the dining room, the bar surfaces are more angular, with wood being the predominant feature. It's an ideal passage from the day's business into the evening's pleasures. Bar hours are from 4 PM until midnight or later (depending on the crowd). If you want to move to Chadfield's in the Hyatt, they are open until 2:00 AM. This Sports Bar is definitely more casual, with peanuts (shells go on the floor), a TV for sporting events and a fireplace.

Fortnums European Cafe

10213 Main Street
Old Bellevue
455-2033

Fortunums has been a favorite of eastsiders for over 12 years. Whether for coffee and pastries or a quiet dinner, the quality never varies. The decor is pink, with lots of paintings on the walls. The mood is continental and very pretty. The age range tends to be thirty to forty, and the clientele is usually friends and business associates during the day. Couples dining quietly are much more common at night, especially Friday night since this is a great place to slow the pace and enjoy a leisurely, cozy meal. You can order coffee and tea, wine, beer and champagne. (Fortnums specializes in offering a new selection of northwest wines every week—all good wines and all priced from $10-$20 per bottle.) You can also indulge in any kind of espresso imagined and the desserts are to die for.

During the nicer months, you can sit outside. But when it's nasty outside, a pleasant afternoon or evening can be spent inside, sipping hot coffee and talking, like a scene from a European movie. Fortnums serves breakfast from 9:00 AM to 11:00 AM, Monday through Saturday, lunch from 11:00 AM to 3:30 PM, Monday through Saturday and dinner from 5:00 PM to 8:30 PM, Friday. They do not take reservations, so you may have to wait for a table. Fortnums accepts all major credit cards and personal checks. Meal prices: $4.00 to $7.00 for lunch and $7.00 to $13.00 for dinner.

The Garden Court

Four Seasons Hotel
411 University Steet
Downtown Seattle
621-1700

Located in the elegant Four Seasons Hotel, the Garden Court looks just like it's name. The windows reach all the way to the very high ceiling and there are plants everywhere. The trees are decorated with little white lights, adding a romantic touch. During the dinner hours, the atmosphere is quiet. Pleasant conversation comes easily while sitting under the trees, next to a waterfall, and enjoying a delicious meal.

On the weekends, the Garden Court has dancing and a jazz and swing band sets the background for a night of fun. A late dinner and dancing is always a near-perfect date option. The dancing begins at 9:00 PM and ends at 1:00 AM; there is no cover charge, but there is a $4.00 minimum. During these hours the age ranges from the mid-forties to the sixties, but during dinner the ages are from thirty and up. The dress is nice to dressy, and dancing clothes are popular on the weekends.

Dinner is served until 11:00 PM. Reservations are strongly suggested. The Garden Court accepts all major credit cards, but no personal checks (that is a hotel rule). Entree prices: $10.00 to $25.00.

The Georgian Room

Four Seasons Hotel
411 University
Downtown Seattle
621-1700

Located in the Four Seasons Hotel, The Georgian is one of the most romantic and elegant restaurants in town. This is the place to really impress your significant other! The decor is "old-world, French chateau, British royalty." A pianist plays soft music for your enjoyment. The mood is quiet elegance, and the setting is perfect for a great meal and sophisticated conversation. The service is as elegant and classy as the surroundings. The dress is nice to dressy, depending on what your plans are for the evening.

The hotel's downtown location makes it a great pre-theater spot for dinner (The Fifth Avenue is right around the corner). Typically the age range is from thirty upwards, with the majority being over forty. Dinner is served until 10:00 PM during the week and until 10:30 PM on the weekends. The Georgian accepts major credit cards, but no personal checks (hotel policy). Reservations are strongly suggested. Entree prices: $20.00 to $30.00

Il Bistro

93A Pike Street
Downtown Seattle
682-3049

Voted one of the Most Romantic Places in Seattle, Il Bistro's European decor is everything you'd expect. The small bistro is romantically decked out with dark wood and white tablecloths. The room is filled with the flickering of candles, and soft jazz plays in the background. The dress ranges from casual to dressy, and either choice is appropriate. The general crowd ranges from the thirties to forties. The menu offers a variety of Italian favorites, and northwest salmon in season.

The bar offers it's own menu of lighter appetizers and snacks, ranging from $5.00 to $10.00. After dinner hours, the bar livens up a bit. The music shifts to Motown, or early sixties and seventies classics.

Dinner hours are from 5:30 PM until 10:00 PM, weeknights, and from 5:30 until 11:00 PM on the weekends. The bar remains open until 2:00 AM. There is a smoking section available. Il Bistro accepts all major credit cards, and personal checks, upon the waiter's discretion. Reservations are suggested for dinner. Entree prices: $10.00-$25.00.

Palisade

2601 W. Marina Place
Elliott Bay Marina
285-1000

The combination of view, architecture and food makes Seattle's newest "see and be seen" restaurant a "must" on your list. Palisade has a spectacular setting at the base of Magnolia, right on Elliott Bay, looking back at the cityscape. (Request side-by-side seating to take full advantage of the water and city view.) The interior is a dramatic artist's rendering of Polynesian and Hawaiian themes. Saltwater pools with fish and starfish and lava rock greet you as you enter the restaurant.

Romance is in the air, as you walk over the waterfalls and ponds, to your table.

At night, the age of the patrons is less obvious than the sense that they are well established. Remember, this is a place to "be seen," so dress accordingly. During the day it's a mixed bag of boaters, seniors and young couples. The meals are beautifully and artistically served on pottery especially designed for Palisade. Piano music can be heard, but not loud enough to disrupt your conversation.

The bar overlooks the restaurant, and has an outdoor deck. On nice nights, this is a great choice for starting or finishing the evening with a Polynesian drink, served in elegant glasses. The bar is open until 12:30 AM, and closes at 11:30 PM on Sundays.

Dinner is served from 5:00 PM to 10:00 PM Sunday through Thursday and from 5:00 PM to 11:00 PM on Friday and Saturday. Palisade accepts major credit cards and personal checks. Entree prices: $10.95 to $28.95. Lunch entrees: $7.95 to $13.95.

The Palm Court

The Westin Hotel
1900 Fifth Avenue
Downtown Seattle
728-1000

Romance is in the air, and in the Westin Hotel's Palm Court. The Palm Court is definitely a "special occasion" evening to share with your sweetheart. The high, secluded booths make for intimate dining. The manager says he, and the waitstaff, are used to witnessing marriage proposals. High school prom dates are also commonplace during the spring months.

The location makes this quiet and elegant restaurant a nice pre-theatre spot. The hotel is a four block walk from the Fifth Avenue Theater, and the Seattle Center is just minutes away by car or monorail. The dress ranges from nice to formal attire, and either one is acceptable, but you and your date should definitely leave the jeans at home for this one! The food is "continental," and not your everyday preparation or presentation. The Palm Court is known for it's superb array of appetizers, both hot and cold.

The staff is extremely friendly and the service is prompt. Dinner is served from 5:30 to 10:00 PM during the week, and from 5:30 to 10:30 on Friday and Saturday. Reservations are a must! Entree prices: $17.00 to $20.00; appetizers in the $6.00 range.

Place Pigalle

81 Pike Street
In the Pike Place Market
Phone: 624-1756

Located in a far corner of the Pike Place Market, this restaurant is quite a surprise. To find it, go behind the fish market near the clock; the restaurant sits out towards the water and below the main level of the market. The black and white checkered floor, wood chairs and white tablecloths create a sophisticated atmosphere. The fresh flowers and candles on each table exude romance. But the view of Elliott Bay eclipses the decor. You can enjoy watching the ships come in and out of the harbor, with Alki Point as background. Honored by the Wine Spectator 1991, the restaurant is well known for it's wine and champagne list.

The menu offers French/Mediterranean dishes, including seafood, beef, lamb, chicken and salads. The age range is mostly mid-thirties and older, with a sophisticated appreciation for food and wine. Place Pigalle is open for lunch from 11:30 AM to 3:00 PM, for dinner from 5:30 PM to 10:00 PM and is closed Sundays. They take all major credit cards and personal checks. Entree prices: $15.95 to $21.95.

Prego

515 Madison Street
Downtown Seattle
583-0300

Perched on the top of the Stouffer Madison Hotel, Prego is an excellent Italian restaurant with a terrific view. The romantic atmosphere hits you from the moment you walk in. The colors are soft and heavy-on-the-mauve. The tables are draped with white tablecloths and the lights are dim. The atmosphere is quiet and relaxed, to encourage an intimate conversation. The incredible views of the city, Elliott Bay and Lake Union make a perfect backdrop. The menu is composed of Italian and Contemporary Northwest cuisine. The entrees look as good as they taste. The age range varies greatly due to the fact the restaurant is located in a hotel, although the typical age is twenty-five and older. Some couples dress up for a meal at Prego's, but office attire is also perfect.

Dinner is served from 5:30 PM to 10:00 PM during the week, and until 11:00 PM on the weekends. Prego accepts all major credit cards and personal checks, with the proper identification. Reservations are strongly suggested, especially when the weather is nice. Entree prices: $20.00 to $25.00.

The Queen Mary

2912 N.E. 55th St.
Just off NE 25th, near University Village
527-2770

Walking into the Queen Mary is like stepping into a room in an English Castle. The floral curtains and elegant chairs create a cozy, yet aristocratic atmosphere. Never mind the royal ambiance, "anything goes" perfectly describes the dress of the customers. People in jeans stop by for an espresso, while a tux and formal clad couple stop in for dinner before the ballet. Afternoon tea is served daily, from 2:00 to 5:00 PM. Tea is $13.95 per person, and is a complete meal of tortes, tarts, scones, crumpets, fruits, sorbets, sandwiches, teacakes, etc... It's a nice idea for an afternoon interlude, as many couples have discovered, and you won't have to plan dinner.

After-dinner interludes are also popular, and the desserts are as delicious as their aroma, which wafts gently in the air. All kinds of espresso and teas are available, day and night. Queen Mary is a wonderful place to just talk; the music is quiet, there are no children running around, and the fare is excellent. Dinner is served Tuesday, Wednesday and Thursday from 5:00 to 9:00 PM, and Friday and Saturday from 5:00 to 10:00 PM. Entree prices: $15.00 to $20.00.

The Salish Lodge

Snoqualmie Falls
Snoqualmie (40 minutes east of Seattle, off I-90)
Toll-free, 1-800-826-6124, or 206-888-2556

Niagara Falls, New York, may be too far away for a romantic dinner, but Snoqualmie Falls is just around the corner. North Bend is a scenic drive from Seattle. The Salish Lodge is located right at the crest of the 268 foot falls, which are actually 100 feet higher than Niagara. You can walk down to the falls, but be sure and wear comfortable shoes. The restaurant serves a 5 course country breakfast, lunch and dinner. The age range changes with the meals as well. Breakfast attracts all ages, while the evening clientele tends towards the thirties and forties.

The breakfast is a big draw, and is served from 7:00 AM to 11:00 AM Monday through Friday and from 7:00 AM to 2:45 PM Saturday and Sunday.   Country Breakfast and Morning Elegance are one price: $18.95.

Lunch is served from 11:30 AM to 2:45 PM Monday through Friday; on Saturday and Sunday, lunch is served from the same times upstairs in the Attic Lounge (age 21 and over only).   Lunch is a nice option, because you still have the light to see the view of the gorge and the river, and it's much less expensive than the evening meal. The dress is casual during the day. Lunch entree prices: $4.50 to $12.50.

Dinner is a more romantic atmosphere, and most couples plan an outside walk to view the falls, which are lit.   Although there is no dress code, diners tend to dress up more at night. The food is "northwest cuisine," and features salmon, quail, rabbit, veal, etc. Dinner is served from 5:00 PM to 9:45 PM every night. Entree prices: $18.00 to $27.00;

Couples over 21 should consider a walk and an appetizer break in the Attic Lounge. This is without question one of the most pleasant views in the area and the comfortable couches and overall cozy country atmosphere makes for a delightful respite from the rush of city and suburban life. Besides a large selection of appetizers, the Lounge can also order up any of the 740 bottled wines and champagnes in the Salish Wine Cellar, 200 of which are from northwest vintners.

Reservations are required, and you will want to make them at least four weeks in advance—sometimes up to 3 months, depending on the season and the meal and the day. The Salish Lodge does not take personal checks, but does accept major credit cards.

Salty's on Alki

1936 Harbor SW
West Seattle Waterfront
937-1600

When you say Salty's is on the water, it is literally *over* the water. Jutting out on the east side of Alki Point, Salty's has one of the most romantic views in the city. You can sit and watch the sunset as it reflects off the Seattle city skyline. Then watch as the lights come on with the rising moon. This breathtaking view is well matched with the interior of Salty's. The decor is simple, yet elegant, with candles on the white-linen-dressed tables. The dress is nice to dressy, and at night mostly dressy.   The typical age range is from thirty to fifty-plus, although high school proms always bring in tables of teens. The specialties are seafood and pasta, with steak and chicken on the menu as well.

Reservations are required, especially if you want a seat right at the window and at sunset. Salty's accepts all major credit cards and personal checks with the proper ID. Dinner is served from 5:00 PM to 10:00 PM Monday through Thursday, from 5:00 PM to 10:30 PM on Friday, from 4:30 PM to 10:30 PM on Saturday, and from 4:30 PM to 10:00 PM on Sunday. Entree prices: $20.00 and up (market prices on some items).

After dinner, take your date on a romantic stroll along the boardwalk. The walk is paved, and high-heel-friendly if you don't overdo it.

Sorrento Hotel

900 Madison Street
Capitol Hill/Downtown
622-6400

Treat your special someone to the most romantic evening of his/her life at the Sorrento Hotel. From the moment you arrive you'll experience old-world elegance. On warm evenings, cocktails and appetizers are served outside on the terrace. You sit beneath umbrella covered tables beside the beautiful Italian fountain, while sipping a cool drink.

If a superb dinner is in the plan, move inside to the Hunt Club restaurant. The ambiance is brick walls, Honduran mahogany wood and soft music. You will find white linen, fresh flowers and candles on every table. It's all designed so that you can gaze into each other's eyes in a romantic setting. Champagne buckets are near by for toasting any celebration. You will find the waitstaff warm and attentive, never stuffy or rushed. The dress tends towards the dressy side. Patrons generally range from the late twenties to seniors. Dinner is served from 5:30 PM to 10:00 PM Sunday through Thursday, and from 5:30 PM to 11:00 PM Friday and Saturday. The Sorrento accepts major credit cards and personal checks with proper ID. Entree prices: $18.59 to $25.00. Reservations are a must! Valet parking is complimentary with brunch, lunch or dinner.

If the evening would not be complete without flowers, call ahead and "Whims," the Sorrento's in-house florist, will make sure you have fresh flowers (a bouquet, a corsage or a single rose) on your table.

After a wonderful meal, why not sit and talk in the Fireside Room? Decorated with velvet love-seats and a huge fireplace, this lounge is like no other in the city. During the cooler months, this is a particularly fine place to sip an after dinner drink, or espresso. The Fireside Lounge is open until 2:00 AM Monday through Saturday, and until midnight on Sundays. There is a pianist to add to the mood Wednesdays through Saturdays.

The Space Needle Restaurant
The Emerald Suite

Seattle Center
443-2100

If you want to make that special someone feel on top of the world, plan dinner in the Emerald Suite at the 500 foot level of the Space Needle. This elegant (and relatively formal at night) restaurant rotates 360 degrees, allowing you to watch the city view turn into lake view, mountain view and Puget Sound view, and then start over again. The clientele ranges from twenties to seniors, and there is a dress code: no jeans, t-shirts or tennis shoes allowed. Reservations are required. Dinner is served Monday through Saturday from 4:00 PM to 10:45 PM, and Sunday from 5:00 PM to 10:45 PM.

For a less formal option—meaning there is no dress code and tourists can be seen in jeans and sneakers during the season—The Space Needle Restaurant is also located at the 500 foot level. Entrees in this adjacent dining room are several dollars less, but the same excellent seafood, beef and chicken specialties are on the menu.

The Space Needle accepts major credit cards and in-state checks with identification. Entree prices: Emerald Suite, $25.00 to $35.00; Space Needle Restaurant, $20.00 to $30.00.

Yarrow Bay Grille

1270 Carillon Point
Kirkland
889-9052

The Yarrow Bay Grille is a very romantic restaurant. In fact, a marriage proposal, or two, is not an uncommon sight during the dinner hour. The enchanting view of Lake Washington can be seen from every table in the restaurant. Located above the Yarrow Bay Marina, you can watch the boating activity over your meal, and then take a stroll along the water's edge. At night, there are candles on the tables and long, white tablecloths. The menu changes daily and includes seafood and steak entrees.

The age range is twenty-five and over, and the atmosphere is quiet and relaxed. Most people are dressed up, but "casual" is acceptable as well. Dinner is served from 5:30 to 10:00 PM Monday through Saturday, and 5:00 to 9:00 PM Sunday. Reservations are suggested, especially if you want to catch the sunset. The Yarrow Bay Grille accepts credit cards and personal checks. Entree prices: $15.00 to $25.00. For reservations call 889-9052.

5

Party Time

Jazz (Daniel's)

Karaoke!

Yarrow Bay, after work

catch the big game at Ram's

meet for "Flat on your beaks"

T his chapter should not need an introduction. If you can't figure out what Party Time means, turn to another area of this book. Not that some of these places aren't relatively sedate at certain times of the day or night, but most of them are ready for action when the crowd moves in for a lively evening. If you want an evening more on the mild side so you can hear each other talk, you will need to read the fine print and pick the places that also offer quiet dining areas or times when the mood is mellow and relaxed. On the other hand, if it's time to shake off the cares of the day, week, or decade...

Azteca Restaurants

Good Mexican food, relatively inexpensive, is the hallmark of this popular local chain of restaurants and lounges. (Still family-owned after 20 years in the northwest, and still dedicated to authentic recipes and "amigos" style hospitality.) The interiors vary, but the general idea is to look like a Mexican Cantina. There are 26 Azteca's in the Seattle area, and each caters to the neighborhood clientele. Some have strolling Mariachis; some are more family oriented than others.

The Shilshole and Lake Union restaurants are right on the water, and are popular with couples, as are the two eastside restaurants and the South Center Azteca. You can expect the noise level to be quiet enough to carry on a conversation, but loud enough to keep things lively. The dress is casual and the age range varies greatly, although the bars do seem to cater to the thirty-plus crowd.

The lounges are comfortable and have a full menu of their own. Entertainment varies from site to site. Karaoke is a big deal in the eastside lounges. Impress your date by singing his/her favorite song. If you don't want to sing, just laugh at everyone who does.

The restaurants keep individual hours, but generally serve from 11:00 AM to 10:30 PM during the week and from 11:00 AM to 11:30 PM on the weekends. They accept all major credit cards and personal checks. Entree prices: $6.00 to $10.00.

Bellevue:	10301 NE 10th Downtown Bellevue 454-8359
	3040 148th NE Overlake 881-8700
Lake Union:	2501 Fairview E. 324-4941
Shilshole:	6017 Seavie NW 789-7373
South Center:	17790 South Center Pkwy 575-0990

Black Angus

1411 156th NE
Crossroads Area/Bellevue
746-1663

The Black Angus chain serves very good food at very good prices. The high booths and dark lighting makes the restaurant a romantic and intimate spot. Yet the dress is casual. The menu is mostly steak and seafood, but chicken and other items are available. The servings are generous and the price is reasonable. Reservations are strongly suggested for weekend nights. Credit cards and personal checks are accepted. Entree prices: $10.00 to $25.00.

The bar at the Bellevue location has a country theme (Black Angus Square Cow Fun Bar) and really jumps at night. Every Thursday and Friday, from 8:00 to 9:00 PM, you can take western dance lessons. If you have never tried western dancing, you'll find learning can be as fun as actually dancing! The average age is the older college graduate, twenty-five to thirty, but the forty to fifty-plus crowd is commonplace.

Note: There are restaurants in Burien, Bremerton, Federal Way and Lynnwood, but only Bellevue and Bremerton have Western dancing.

The Bookstore

Alexis Hotel
1007 1st Avenue
Downtown Seattle
624-4844

The Bookstore is a bar, coffee shop and bookstore. What a combination! The walls are decorated with books, including a large selection of cookbooks which are for sale. Newspapers are also available to read over your drink or espresso. The menu includes salads, burgers and sandwiches—mostly light items. Starbucks and Seattle's Best Coffee are served, along with wine, beer and mixed drinks.

The atmosphere is upscale, with a little bit of "soho" mixed in. There is soft music playing, but the majority of the low-key background noise comes from conversation. A thirty-plus crowd makes up the majority of the clientele. The Bookstore is open from 11:30 AM, until 2:00 AM, making this an ideal place to drop in after a show. Smoking is allowed, but there is no designated section available. Parking can be found either in the Alexis Hotel parking garage, or on the street. The

Bookstore takes major credit cards and checks. Entree prices: $5.00 to $8.00 and the drinks are moderate to expensive.

Casa U Betcha

2212 First Avenue
Seattle/Belltown Area
441-1989

Casa U Betcha is a Mexican style cantina with brightly colored walls and tables. The atmosphere is lively and the crowd ranges from twenty-one to early thirties. The loud, to extremely loud, noise level is either a plus or a minus, depending on how much you have to talk about! Outdoor seating is available for those warm summer nights, and the adjoining bar is open until 1:30 AM.

The food is Mexican, spicy, and served in large portions. Dinner is served seven nights a week, from 5:00 until 11:00 PM. There is a smoking section available upon request. Entree prices: $8.00 to $15.00. They accept all major credit cards but no personal checks.

Casa U Betcha also has a very wild bar, serving beer ($2.50-$3.50) and an assortment of Casa Cocktails, including Margaritas ($4.50-$5.00). Karaoke provides a great source of entertainment on Sunday and Monday nights, for those with (and without) musical talents.

Cutter's Bayhouse

2001 Western
Pike Place Market
448-4884

A perfect way to end a stroll through the Pike Place Market is a meal, or drink, at Cutter's Bayhouse. The restaurant looks out at Elliot Bay and Puget Sound beyond. The atmosphere is light and lively, with an open kitchen and high ceilings. Cutter's 100% non-smoking environment makes it a haven for those offended by cigarette smoke. The menu includes a little of everything, from salads to steaks, though seafood is a specialty and comes fresh from the nearby fish markets. Cutter's serves Tom Stockley's carefully selected wines.

Although you'll see all ages here, the crowd tends toward the young professional. The noise level does tend to rise quickly, especially on weekend nights. The bar is a very active place, and the sounds of conversation spill over into the busy restaurant. However, one can still carry on a conversation for two. Dinner is served until 11:00 PM and until 1:30 AM in the lounge. Parking is available in the Market Place garage as well as on-street parking. Reservations are strongly suggested. Cutter's accepts major credit cards and local checks. Entree prices: $10.00 to $20.00.

Da Vinci's

89 Kirkland Avenue
Downtown Kirkland
889-9000

Couples love the boisterous atmosphere of Da Vinci's as much as the food. The house specialties are pizza, pasta and cocktails. The place looks like something right out of New York City. The walls are covered with graffiti and posters. The bar opens up onto Kirkland's main street, affording terrific people-watching opportunities. The restaurant also has an outdoor section on the side street headed towards Lake Washington and the Kirkland marina. The age range varies with the season and the night. During the summer you'll find more college kids, home for summer vacation. The school year draws an older crowd, and the locals. Generally, the age range is twenty-one to forty-plus. Whatever your age, if you like to have fun, you'll love Da Vinci's. Wednesdays and Thursdays feature Karaoke in the bar, and on Fridays and Saturdays it is in the restaurant. The restaurant is open from 11:30 to 1:00 AM (ish!). The bar hours vary, depending on the crowd. Da Vinci's accepts MasterCard, Visa, American Express and personal checks. Entree prices: $6.00 to $9.00. Pizzas: $8.00 to $18.00.

Daniel's Broiler

8th at Bellevue Way
Bellevue Place
462-4662

Located in the same complex that houses the Hyatt Hotel, but atop the Seafirst/Bellevue Place building, Daniel's Broiler is one of the few "view" restaurants in Bellevue. The high wood booths and well-spaced tables make for a romantic setting, and at night there are candles on the tables. The view of Bellevue and Lake Washington is spectacular, and on a clear night you can see Seattle. The atmosphere is quiet and relaxed. The food is very good.

The adjoining bar is mellow, and every Sunday night features a popular Jazz Showcase. If you and your friend love jazz, every Sunday from 7:00 PM to 11:00 PM you can enjoy live music. The Sunday Jazz Showcase can get very busy, so plan to arrive early.

The casual yet upscale atmosphere of Daniel's Broiler draws a thirty to fifty-ish crowd. It's definitely a place to impress a date without overdoing it. Dinner is served from 5:30 to 10:00 PM Monday through Thursday, from 5:30 to 11:00 PM Friday and Saturday, and from 5:00 to 10:00 PM on Sunday. The dress is eclectic; some people are dressed up, others are very casual. You won't feel out of place in either choice. Entree prices: $15.00 to $25.00. Major credit cards and personal checks accepted.

The Duchess

2728 NE 55th
University Village area
527-8606

The Duchess—Juke Joint, Sports Bar and Eatery—is perfect for all you sports lovers out there. Established in 1934, this tav is very popular with U.W. students, especially the "Greeks." However, don't let this scare you away! The Duchess is also an "after game" hang out for many of the local business-sponsored sports teams around Seattle. Typically, the crowd is twenty-one to forty-ish (you must be at least twenty-one, and ID is required). The Duchess has television sets all over the bar, pool tables and dart boards.

The dress is casual, and the atmosphere is medium to loud. Definitely a spot for a casual date, the Duchess doesn't offer intimate surroundings. Things get even more active during the Husky Football season. In fact, the Duchess opens early on Husky game days (8:30 AM). The regular hours are from 4:00 PM to 2:00 AM Monday through Friday, 11:00 AM to 2:00 AM Saturday and 11:00 AM to 12:00 AM Sunday. The menu includes appetizers and burgers, and the bar serves beer by the pitcher. Entree prices: $4.50 Appetizers: $2.00 to $5.00.

Dukes Restaurants

The aim of the Duke's group of restaurants is to provide good food, good service, and a casual and fun place to hang out with your friends. The restaurants are classed by types (bar and grilles, chowder-houses and the fish house), and there are some differences which you may want to consider when making your plans. The restaurants accept major credit cards and personal checks.

The bar and grille's are located in Bellevue (10116 NE 8th; 455-5775) and Queen Anne (236 1st W.; 283-4400). The Pioneer Square restaurant is somewhat similar (83 King; 622-6743). The emphasis is upon value, reasonable prices for good size portions. The atmosphere is somewhat sports oriented and the bars are almost always lively. The crowd is usually sophisticated and from thirty to fifty-plus. The menu offers everything from hamburgers to lobster. Entree prices: $8.00 to $20.00. Reservations are suggested, especially for weekend dinners.

The chowder houses, located at Lake Union (901 Fairview N.; 382-9963) and Green Lake (7850 Green Lake Dr. N.; 522-4908), are a little more casual (though none of the Duke's restaurants should be considered formal). The age range is from college grads to mid-thirties—the young professional crowd. The chowder houses are good places to go kick back with a good friend and catch a sports event. Entree prices: $6.00 to $12.00.

Duke's Lake Union (1111 Fairview N.; 292-9402) is located right on the lake, so the view is incredible. Summer months are especially popular. The menu is similar to the bar and grille offerings, plus some seafood and smoked chicken options. Entree prices: $8.00 to $20.00.

Duke's Fifth Avenue Fish House (623-2296) is located right under the Fifth Avenue Theater and attracts pre-theater diners. Theater nights are crowded, and the dress tends to be more formal. The age range depends on the theater productions, but generally thirty-five to fifty-plus. Reservations are a must on theater nights. Entree prices: $8.00 to $20.00.

Ernie's Bar and Grille

2411 Alaskan Way/Edgewater Hotel
Waterfront
728-7000

Located in the city's only waterfront hotel, The Edgewater, Ernie's Bar and Grille is the only lounge of its type in Seattle. The entire restaurant and bar is built on pilings, so you are actually sitting over the water. The giant picture windows reach from floor to ceiling. You feel like you are on a cruise ship. The restaurant is decorated in soft greens and light wood. There is a brick fireplace, and the atmosphere is mellow. Typically the age range is from twenty-five and older, however prom dates are a common sight during spring. The dress tends to be on the dressy side, and reservations are a must.

The bar is more casual and very low key. It has the same large windows and sweeping view of Puget Sound and Alki Point as the restaurant. You can sit and enjoy a drink, while watching the ferry boats come in and out of Elliott Bay. The bar features piano, so the music is not overbearing. Tuesday nights are "blues in the bar" selections from 8:30 PM to 12:30 AM.

Dinner is served in the restaurant from 5:00 PM to 9:30 PM every night. Parking is validated by the hotel if you park in the hotel lot. Ernie's Bar and Grille accepts all major credit cards and personal checks. Entree prices: $11.95 to $18.95 (market prices are subject to change on some items).

Espresso Roma

420 University Avenue
University District
632-6001

Located right on "The Ave" near the University of Washington, Espresso Roma is a great people watching spot. The cement walls are covered with art, posters and flyers. If you just want to casually get to know each other over a cup of coffee, there's always a lot to look at and talk about, so conversation comes easily. The pleasant hum of conversation inside serves as the backdrop for the constant moving theater out on the street.

The service is casual: you order at the counter and bus your own table. You can sit and talk, or people-watch from the outdoor deck. The deck is situated almost on the sidewalk, so you won't miss any of the activity. The ages of the patrons varies, but the majority are college age and in their twenties. Espresso Roma is open from 7:00 AM to 11:00 PM Monday through Friday, from 8:00 AM to 11:00 PM Saturday, and from 9:00 AM to 11:00 PM Sunday. They do not take credit cards or checks: cash only, please. Espresso prices: $1.00 to $2.00.

The Keg

The Keg is a great spot to take a date, whether a first date or someone you know well. The restaurant has semi-secluded booths and tables, surrounded by dark wood. The warm and friendly service will make you feel right at home. The dress is generally casual. The food is moderately priced, so it needn't be an expensive evening. But don't let the prices fool you. The Keg serves some of the best steak and seafood around. They also have an outstanding salad bar.

The Keg is open from 11:00 AM to 1:30 AM Monday through Friday, from 11:30 AM to 1:30 AM Saturday, and from 9:30 AM to 12:30 PM Sundays. These late hours make it a popular late dinner spot. The typical age range is eighteen to forty, but all ages are seen. The Keg accepts Visa, MasterCard, American Express and personal checks. Reservations are suggested, especially on weekend nights. Entree prices: $10.00 to $20.00.

The lounge sections can range from quiet and uncrowded to mobbed and noisy, depending on the hour, the night and the decibel level of the music. Weekly drink specials are a feature.

The Factoria Keg is across the street from Factoria Cinemas, making "dinner and a movie" very convenient. The Keg near the University of Washington, in the Metro Center, has a little different decor, but the same great food. The Metro theaters are just around the corner in the same complex.

Locations:
    3600 128th Se, Factoria, Bellevue (644-9700)
    Off 45th at Roosevelt, University district, Seattle (547-6525)
    10600 NE 38th Place, Kirkland (822-5131)
    6620 NE 181st, Kenmore (485-7533)

Kells Irish Restaurant and Pub

1916 Post Alley
Pike Place Market
728-1916

Kells, tucked away on Post Alley, is a traditional Irish pub, decorated in the traditional Irish manner. This translates into dark wood, dim light and a friendly mood. The walls are covered with paintings and photographs of Ireland. The menu features traditional Irish meals, including: Hibernian Salads, Dublin Coddle, Irish Stew and Ethna's Irish Breads (to name a few).

The adjoining bar is an authentic Irish pub, with good ol' Irish beers. Irish music is always playing, but there is also live Irish music and dancing on certain evenings. The dress is casual and the atmosphere relaxed. Everyone from any age range is welcome at Kells, twenty-one and up in the pub. Kells has it's regulars, who are in the thirty-plus range, but on weekend nights, college students occupy the pub as well.

Outdoor seating is available during the summer months, which adds to the overall European flavor. Dinner is served until 10:00 PM, Monday through Saturday. Reservations are strongly recommended for Friday and Saturday nights. When asked what time the pub closed, the Irish Hostess replied, "When everyone gets tired!" Kells accepts Visa, MasterCard and local checks. Entree prices: $10.00 to $15.00.

Lake Bellevue Cafe

23 Lake Bellevue
Midlakes/Bellevue
455-4442

Lake Bellevue Cafe is located on Bellevue's beautiful, and only, urban lake. It can be either a lively *or* relaxing choice for a date, depending on the time of day and day of the week that you go. The big windows and the plants give the restaurant a light and airy decor. Dinner is generally quiet, comfortable and relaxing. The average age is from twenty-eight to fifty-plus, during the week, and from twenty-one to thirty-plus on the weekends.

The bar really hops at night! During the week, it is primarily a "young professional crowd," and on the weekends, the college crowd moves in. Dinner is served from 5:00 PM to 10:00 PM Monday through Thursday, from 5:00 PM to 11:00 PM Friday, from 4:00 PM to 1:00 AM Saturday and 4:00 PM to 9:00 PM on Sunday. The dress is pretty much full range, though on the upscale side, and the bar does have a dress code. Lake Bellevue Cafe accepts all major credit cards and personal checks, with ID. Reservations are suggested. Entree prices: $7.00 to $15.00.

Latitude 47

1232 Westlake Avenue N.
West Lake Union
284-1047

The decor and location of Latitude 47 makes you think nautical. The giant windows give you the sensation that you can almost reach out and touch Lake Union. Bamboo chairs and plants create the exotic flavor of a sea-side paradise. A candlelit table for two, right on the water's edge, awaits you. The specialty is seafood, and their claim to fame is having "Seattle's Freshest Seafood." The dress leans towards dressy, and the typical age range is twenty-one to thirty-something. The restaurant serves dinner from 5:00 PM to 9:30 PM weeknights, and from 5:00 PM to 10:00 PM on the weekends.

Latitude 47 also has a hopping lounge, called Club 47. Here you can enjoy videos, dancing and large screen sports viewing. Club 47 is open until 2:00 AM and is a great place to dance the night away. The dress tends to be more casual than the restaurant, but no shorts allowed. There is a $3.00 cover and Karaoke is featured every Thursday night from 7:30 PM to 10:30 PM. On Wednesday and Sundays you can try Latin Dancing from 9:00 PM to 1:30 AM. Lambada!

Reservations are suggested, especially on weekends. They accept major credit cards and personal checks. Entrees: $15.00 to $20.00.

Lox, Stock and Bagel

4552 University Way N.
University District
Phone: 634-3144

A true U.W. gathering spot, the Lox, Stock and Bagel is a fun, and inexpensive, place to spend an evening. The atmosphere is casual, with palm trees and bright pictures as decorations. The menu has something for everyone, from ethnic to burgers and salads. Typically, the clientele is twenty-one to thirty; depending on the night, the crowd can be older. Music nights are Wednesday, Friday and Saturday, and the cover is only $2.00 Friday and Saturdays (Wednesday is free). Music nights attract the most couples, as well as the greatest age range, depending upon the group playing. Lox, Stock and Bagel claims to have the cheapest music in town. You and your companion can enjoy an evening of great music, and still have enough money left to enjoy the food and drink. The music is typically loud, so don't anticipate a quiet, romantic atmosphere. However, do expect lots of noisy fun. Lox, Stock and Bagel is open until 2:00 AM every night and accepts Visa, MasterCard, and personal checks with the proper ID. Entree prices: $5.00 to $8.00; well drinks and beers are only $2.00.

McCormick & Schmick's

1103 First Avenue
Downtown Seattle
623-5500

Located in the heart of downtown Seattle, McCormick and Schmick's is a lively place to take a date or to meet a special friend after work. The restaurant has a casual and comfortable appeal which also makes it a nice "get to know you" place. The atmosphere comes alive with the "after work" crowd and is a "happening" late night spot as well. Typically, the age range is from twenty-five to forty-five—the professional crowd. The dress is business attire for those coming straight from work, and casual for those who had time to change.

McCormick and Schmick's has a late bar menu, which includes drink specials, from 11:00 PM to closing (which is sometime after 1:00 AM). Happy hour light menu specials in the bar are a great deal at $1.95 (calamari, oyster shooters, chicken wings, mussels, burgers, fettucine...), and are served from 3:00 PM to 6:00 PM on weekdays, and from 5:00 to 6:00 PM on weekends.

The dining room specializes in seafood and the menu changes daily to offer fresh specials. The decor of the dining room is casual, with a lot of wood and brass. McCormick and Schmick's can get noisy, so don't plan an intimate getaway here. Do plan on a great meal, a lot of fun and a busy atmosphere. Reservations are suggested, especially on weekend nights. They accept personal checks, AMEX, MasterCard, and Visa. Entree prices: $10.00 to $20.00.

Pioneer Square

North of the Kingdome,
South of Downtown,
West of the International District

Taking your favorite person out on the town? Planning a night of food, music and dancing? Some of the bars in Pioneer Square have gotten together to make you a great deal. A cover charge of $7.00 is your admission to seven bars. This offer is available Friday and Saturday nights only. The typical age range during the evening music scene is from twenty-one to thirty-five-plus, and everyone is ready to party! The dress is casual, but to impress (especially the opposite sex). The mood changes as fast as you switch bars. Generally, the atmosphere is loud to very loud, with lots of conversation and an equal or greater amount of music.

The hustle and bustle of the crowds makes Pioneer Square a great option for first dates and dancing partners, but probably not your best choice for an intimate evening for two. The bars take cash and credit, but generally no checks, so come prepared. Here are some of the bars which are included in this special deal:

Larry's Greenfront Lounge
209 1st Avenue S.
624-7665

Old Timer's Cafe
620 1st Avenue S.
623-9800

New Orleans Restaurant
114 1st Avenue S.
622-2563

Merchants Cafe
109 Yesler Way
624-1515

Swan Cafe and Nightclub
608 1st Avenue S.
343-5288

The Fenix Cafe
111 Yesler Way
447-1514

Doc Maynard's
610 1st Avenue S.
628-4649

Ponti Seafood Grille

3014 3rd North
North Queen Anne/Near Fremont Bridge
284-3000

The atmosphere alone is reason enough to visit Ponti's. Located right on the channel leading to Lake Union and directly in view of the Fremont Bridge, this seafood grille is a great escape. Lunch or Sunday brunch are excellent options The boating activity in the narrow channel below is reminiscent of the canal scene in Amsterdam, and the Fremont bridge is raised now and again for drama. In nice weather, you can also enjoy the early evening with a drink and appetizer outside on either the deck or patio.

For dinner, the white linen tablecloths and dim lights set a romantic mood. Ponti's is a quiet, upscale setting. The bar is smallish, but very lively at night. There is a big fireplace at one end, adding a cozy touch during the winter months. The age ranges from twenty-five to forty-ish, and the dress is "well put-together." If you are simply enjoying the outside deck, then casual, but not unkempt, dress is appropriate.

Dinner is served from 5:30 PM to 10:00 PM, Sunday through Thursday and from 5:30 PM to 11:00 PM, Friday and Saturday. The Bar is open until 1:00 AM on the weeknights and until 2:00 AM on the weekends. Ponti suggests reservations. Entree prices: $10.95 to $19.95.

Ram Cafe and Sports Bar

4730 University Village
University District
525-3565

For the sports loving couple, Ram's is a great place. The walls are covered with sporting photos and the atmosphere is as fun as cheering for the home team. TVs in every room broadcast sporting events all day and all night. Close to the University of Washington, the college crowd makes up the majority of the customers. However, there is a regular crowd which ranges from thirty and up, so it's not just a college party.

The adjoining bar always hops and serves the full menu as well. Happy hour runs from 3:00 to 6:00 PM and from 10:00 PM to 1:30 AM. Karoake is a big hit Tuesdays and Saturdays, from 9:30 PM to 1:30 AM. The restaurant's noise level is moderate to loud, depending on the night (weekends are louder). The bar can get louder yet, especially with the Karoake.

Dinner is served until midnight Monday through Saturday, and until 11:00 PM on Sunday. The bar is open until 2:00 AM *daily*. This late night dinner service makes Ram's a great place to go after a movie or sporting event. They accept all major credit cards and personal checks. Entree prices: $6.00 to $8.00.

Red Robin

Eastlake E. & Fuhrman E.
University District (south of the bridge)
323-0917

Located up on the bluff, overlooking Portage Bay, the "original" Red Robin has been a popular casual date destination since 1943. From humble origins as the closest tav to the campus, this Red Robin hatched a full-fledged franchise operation. The tavern-now-restaurant is decorated with bright colors and plants, and the menu is extensive; there's a lot to look at, if you are lean on conversational topics.

The house specialty is off-beat burgers and wacky drinks. Your companion may or may not be impressed by someone who orders a Rookie Magic or Later Alligator, or the all-time favorite, Flat on Your Beak. The bar has tables which sit beneath greenhouse windows, overlooking the water, and there is outdoor seating on the deck. You can watch the boats below, and maybe see the University Bridge open for the big yachts. Happy Hour is from 3:00 PM to 6:00 PM and 10:00 PM to closing, and it can get pretty loud during this time.

The age range is from eighteen to thirty-something on weekend nights (U.W. students make up the majority) and a little older during the week. The hours are from 11:00 AM to 11:00 PM Monday through Thursday, from 11:00 AM to 1:00 AM Friday and Saturday, and from 11:00 AM to 11:00 PM Sunday. The Red Robin does not take reservations. Visa, MasterCard and AMEX are all taken, but no personal checks. Entree prices: $4.99 to $8.99.

Roanoke Park Place Tavern

2409 10th E.
Capitol Hill
324-5882

You are looking for a nice, but fun bar to just kick back and have a beer with a date or a good friend. The Roanoke Tavern is an excellent choice. The atmosphere is very casual and it does, indeed, look like a bar. However, this tavern is popular with locals who strive to keep their neighborhood hang-out a safe place. The Roanoke attracts college students, as well as the neighbors and sports teams. This mix adds to the tavern flavor.

The menu features burger and snack items, served until 10:00 PM. The bar itself is open every day from 12:00 PM to 2:00 AM. The age range is from twenty-one to forty-and-up; typically the college group shows up later, after 9:00 PM. They accept credit cards and personal checks, with the proper ID. Entree prices: $4.00 to $7.00. Beer: $1.50 to $2.25 (glass), $1 to $2.25 (glass), $1.75 to $2.75 (bottles) and pitchers $5.00 to $7.50. Wine: $2.00 to $4.00 (glass).

The Roost

102 NW Gilman Blvd.
Issaquah
392-5550

The Roost (related to the Mick McHugh restaurants like The Roaster in Kirkland) is named after Issaquah's first business establishment, a saloon. At that time (1887) Issaquah was called Squak. Today's Roost is both restaurant and lounge. The dress, like the atmosphere, is casual and relaxed and the meals are inexpensive. The noise level is medium to quiet, except in the bar. The typical age range is about twenty five and up—older than college age. The bar is a fun place to have a drink, with a happy hour from 3:00 to 8:00 PM Monday through Friday. Dinner is served until 9:00 PM Monday through Thursday, and until 10:00 PM on Saturday and Sunday. Issaquah has progressed well beyond it's humble beginnings, but is still a little town which you and your companion might want to explore together. There are country roads, lots of hiking and biking opportunities not far away, and the ski slopes 45 minutes east. It's easy to make a day of it and end up at the Roost. They accept major credit cards and personal checks. Reservations are recommended. Entree prices: $6.00 to $20.00.

T.G.I. Fridays

505 Parkplace
Parkplace Shopping Center
Downtown Kirkland
828-3743

T.G.I. Fridays is a great place for a fun evening no matter what night of the week it is. This is an ideal place to bring a first date, simply because there is so much activity that's its easy to join in. If you are with a long-time love, you may find this place a little on the loud side, but you can always sit closer together.

There are lots of appetizers and exotic drinks. The menu has something for everyone: salads, burgers, steaks, chicken, pasta and fajitas (that's naming only a few of the selections). The dress is casual, but not grubby. Typically, the age range is from twenty-one to fifty-plus on the weekends, and from thirty and older during the weeknights. Outdoor seating is available when the weather permits.

T.G.I. Fridays is open until midnight Monday through Thursday, until 2:00 AM Friday and Saturday, and until 1:00 AM on Sundays. These late hours make it perfect to stop in after a movie, especially since the Parkplace Cineplex is right next door. You can make it dinner and a movie, without moving your car. (For more information on The Parkplace, see page 29.) T.G.I. Fridays accepts all major credit cards, but no personal checks. Entree prices: $7.00 to $10.00.

Tlaquepaque Bar

1122 Post Alley
Pike Place Market
467-8226

The name Tlaquepaque comes from a Mexican city famous as a center for artists and craftspersons. So what does this have to do with a bar? Well, consider that Tequila is made from the agave (cactus) plants that are plentiful in the outskirts of Tlaquepaque...you get the point. Plan on an evening of fiesta time at this Mexican Cantina. The atmosphere is loud and wild, so don't plan on a quiet dinner for two. However, do plan to enjoy great Mexican food in a fun bar. The typical age range is from twenty-one to thirty-something and the dress is very casual.

Dinner is served from 5:00 PM to 10:00 PM Monday through Thursday, 5:00 PM to 11:30 Friday, from 2:00 PM to 11:30 PM Saturday and from 2:00 PM to 10:00 PM Sunday. The bar is open until 11:00 PM Monday through Thursday, until 1:00 AM Friday and Saturday, and until 10:00 PM Sunday. Tlaquepaque accepts all major credit cards and personal checks with proper ID. Entree prices: $8.00 to $14.00.

Volcano Cafe

90 Madison (south of the Alexis Hotel)
Downtown Seattle
682-5019

The name used to say it all...but now it's a remnant of the past "Pacific Rim" theme. This comfortable, eclectic restaurant/cafe/music club is an excellent first date, long-term relationship renewal opportunity, or bring the group option. The live music ranges from progressive folk to acoustic rock 'n' roll to jazz quartets. Check the local newspaper listings or give them a call if you are particular about which type of local group you like to enjoy.

The menu is casual (as is the dress code) and features burgers, sandwiches, south-of-the-border selections, salads and soups. There's a full bar, and a good selection of northwest brews on tap. Though the lights are dim, the noise level can rise with conversation and music. Happy hour runs from 4:00 to 7:00 PM. The crowd tends to be twenties to forty-and-counting. Smoking is allowed anywhere in the restaurant and bar. The Volcano Cafe accepts all major credit cards but no personal checks. Dinner is served nightly from 5:00 until 10:30 PM. Entree prices: $5.00 to $7.00.

The Yarrow Bay Beach Cafe

1270 Carillon Point
Kirkland
889-0303

Located below the Yarrow Bay Grille, the Beach Cafe is more casual and the accent is on noisy fun. The atmosphere is lively, with bright colors and flags adding a nautical touch. Outdoor seating is available out on the deck, when the weather permits. Whether it's your first, or one hundred and first, date, this is a good place to kick back and unwind at the edge of Lake Washington. The age range is from twenty to forty, but both younger and older will feel comfortable eating here.

The bar is lively, and attracts a crowd ranging from twenty-one to thirty-ish. Dinner is served from 5:00 to 10:00 PM Sunday through Thursday, and from 5:00 to 11:00 PM Friday and Saturday. The bar is open from 11:00 AM to 12:00 AM Sunday through Thursday, and from 11:00 to 1:30 AM Friday and Saturday. Entree prices: $6.00 to $15.00. Reservations are suggested, depending on the weather.

Broadway

The great thing about dating in Seattle is the diversity of the people who live and work here. Broadway is one of those places where all kinds of people, food and cultures are expressed. This makes for a great place to take a date because the many Broadway offerings suit every mood and taste. You can park the car at one end of the strip, then wander along until you find something of interest. Here are a few spots which are especially popular with couples. They are listed from north to south as you walk down Broadway.

Deluxe Bar and Grille

625 Broadway E.
324-9697

The Deluxe is one of Broadway's oldest hangouts (opened in 1962), and continues to serve some of the best burgers in town. It also makes a perfect first date, or spot to hit for a nightcap after a movie or play. The establishment is small and comfortable, with some outdoor seating. They do not take any reservations, so it is first come, first served. The music is medium to loud, and there is always conversation noise. The crowd ranges from twenty-one to thirty-five-ish and tends to be very lively. The hours are from 11:00 AM to 2:00 AM Monday through Friday, and from 10:00 AM to 2:00 AM on Saturday and Sunday. Entree prices: $6.00. Beer: $1.00 to $3.00.

Cafe Cielo

611 Broadway E.
324-9084

The newly re-decorated Cafe Cielo is a very pleasant Italian restaurant. A kind of "there to see and be seen" place, the dress is "to impress." The atmosphere is relaxed, and the decor is comfortable, yet attractive. Solo jazz piano is featured Thursday, Friday and Saturday nights, and the crowd digs the music. The age range is from twenty-one to fifty-plus, and everything in between. There is some outdoor seating, when weather permits. Dinner is served from 4:00 PM to Midnight and the bar is open until 2:00 AM on the weekends. Cafe Cielo accepts credit cards and personal checks, with valid Washington ID. Reservations are recommended. Entree prices: $8.00 to $15.00.

Starbucks Coffee

516 Broadway E.
323-7888

Starbucks brews some of the best coffee in town, not to mention the scrumptious pastries they serve with it! This particular Starbucks has limited seating, and most orders are to go. You can get an espresso for your trip down Broadway, or you can enjoy the quiet atmosphere. Starbucks is open from 6:30 AM to 9:00 PM Monday through Thursday, from 6:30 AM to 10:30 PM on Friday, from 7:00 AM to 10:30 PM on Saturday and from 7:30 AM to 9:00 PM on Sunday. They take major credit cards and personal checks. Espresso prices: $1.50 to $2.50.

La Cocina and Cantina

432 Broadway E.
323-1676

How about Mexican food, or maybe just a Margarita at La Cocina and Cantina? The restaurant opens up onto the street when the weather is nice. All ages feel right at home here, and the atmosphere is pure fun. The food is very authentic and so are the surroundings. The hours are from 11:00 AM to 12:00 AM Monday through Thursday, from 11:00 AM to 1:00 AM Friday, from 11:30 AM to 1:00 AM Saturday and from 11:30 AM to 11:00 PM Sunday. La Cocina and Cantina accepts credit cards, but no personal checks. No reservations are needed. Entree prices: $4.00 to $8.00.

Dilettante Chocolate

416 Broadway E.
329-6463

Does the name spark some interest? If so, then you'll love what is inside. Dilettante Chocolate is a combination chocolate store, espresso bar and cafe. At night, the restaurant is lit by candles at every table and the setting is very romantic, but still casual. You can sip espresso and share a hot fudge sundae, while engaging in serious intellectual debate or gazing quietly into each other's eyes. There are no reservations, and you may have to wait for a table, especially on weekend nights. The age range is typically twenty-five and older, but pre-twenty-one couples also frequent this place. Dilettante is open from 10:00 AM to midnight on weekdays and until 1:00 AM on weekends. Entree prices: $5.00 to $10.00. They accept major credit cards and personal checks. Espresso prices: $1.50 to $3.00.

The Broadway Market

401 Broadway E.
322-1610

A Broadway version of Bellevue Square and The Pike Place Market, the Broadway Market shopping center is unique in our area. Granted, it has all the usual mall amenities like stores and food, but it also has a movie theater, a salon called Billy Buck's Salon and Gallery, a half-price ticket outlet and numerous funky stands. Seattle Floral is on the corner, if you want to buy your date a special gift. The Broadway Market is a great place to spend time wandering around before a movie, or just browsing any time. The hours are from 10:00 AM to 9:00 PM Monday through Saturday and from 12:00 PM to 6:00 PM Sunday.

(For more information on the theater, see page 26)

Hamburger Mary's

401 Broadway E.
In the Broadway Market
325-6565

The funky atmosphere of Hamburger Mary's makes it popular with couples of all ages. They serve everything from sandwiches to steaks, plus a vegetarian menu, and of course, burgers. The adjoining bar brings in it's own crowd, attracted by special events like Aloha Fridays, featuring exotic drink specials. The decor is a mis-match of colors and themes, with an emphasis on fifties style. The age range is from twenty to forty and the dress is casual. The hours are from 10:00 AM to 1:00 AM Monday through Wednesday, 10:00 AM to 2:00 AM Thursday and Friday, 9:00 AM to 2:00 AM Saturday and 9:00 AM to 1:00 AM Sunday. Hamburger Mary's accepts credit cards, but no personal checks.

Broadway New American Grille

314 Broadway E.
328-7000

Perfect for you late night diners, the Broadway New American Grille serves a full menu until 1:00 AM on weekend nights. The glass roof and big windows give the restaurant a light, airy and casual atmosphere. Menu options include burgers, salads, pastas. The noise level can range from medium to loud, depending on the night and crowd. The age range is from twenty-one to thirty-five-ish, and there is an adjoining bar. The hours are from 11:00 AM to 2:00 AM Monday through Friday and from 10:00 AM to 2:00 AM on Saturday and Sunday. No reservations are necessary. Visa, MasterCard, AMEX and personal checks accepted. Entree prices: $5.00 to $8.00.

Angel's Thai Cuisine

235 Broadway E.
328-0515

Those who appreciate Thai food, or like trying new cuisines, will want to stop in at Angel's Thai. The atmosphere is casual. When you walk in, you can watch the food being prepared in the open kitchen. The food is authentic Thai, but the restaurant has been Americanized. The noise level includes kitchen sounds, as well as quiet music. The age ranges from twenty to fifty-plus. Angel's is open from 11:30 AM to 10:30 PM Monday through Thursday, 11:30 AM to 11:00 PM Friday, 12:00 PM to 11:00 PM Saturday and 12:00 PM to 10:00 PM Sunday. Angel's accepts major credit cards, but no personal checks. Entree prices: $8.00 to $10.00.

Charlie's

217 Broadway E.
323-2535

The only thing old-fashioned about Charlie's is the decor. This hip restaurant attracts all ages from eighteen to sixty. (The bar tends to be twenty-one to fifty.) Charlie's also serves very late, which makes it a popular late-night spot. The dress ranges from casual to dressy, depending on a couple's evening plans. The menu selections are classic "American," meaning steaks, roast beef, pasta, salads, etc. Charlie's accepts credit cards and personal checks, and reservations are not necessary. Dinner is served until 2:00 AM Monday through Thursday, until 3:00 AM on Friday and until 1:00 AM Saturday and Sunday. Entree prices: $6.00 to $8.00.

Testa Rossa

210 Broadway E.
328-0878

Are you a pizza lover? Has your date ever experienced stuffed pizza? If you answered "yes," and then "no," you must try Testa Rossa. The atmosphere and patrons can best be described as "arty." The plaid tablecloths and tile floors are totally hip. The age range is from twenty-five to fifty-plus, but younger couples frequent the place as well. The hours are from 11:00 AM to 11:00 PM Monday through Thursday, from 11:00 AM to midnight Friday and Saturday, and from 1:00 PM to 10:00 PM Sunday. Testa Rossa accepts major credit cards and personal checks. Pizza prices: $15.00 to $22.00.

Espresso Roma

202 Broadway E.
324-1866

Tucked away in a quiet corner, you will find Roma Espresso. This coffee shop is the perfect place to sit and carry on a quiet conversation. The crowd is typically twenty and over, and is generally an intellectual and artistic group. The tables seat two or three, so a couple can enjoy a little privacy. The walls are decorated with posters and flyers of cultural events. Espresso Roma is open until 11:00 PM or 12:00 AM, depending on the crowd. They do not take credit cards, or checks: cash only. Espresso prices: $1.00 to $2.00.

T here must be an unlimited number of ways to play together in the Puget Sound area. For starters, our list includes both indoor and outdoor ideas, with a sampling of activities ranging from bowling to rock-climbing. You soon learn what happens when the gauntlet is down and the challenge begins. This is especially helpful in assessing the likelihood that the relationship will move successfully into more cooperative stages. Not that all play is competitive: dancing and canoeing are among the non-competitive activities for lovers and friends.

Billiards

Jillian's Billiard Club and Cafe
731 Westlake North
Just off SW Lake Union
223-0300

You don't have to be an expert pool player to enjoy a night at Jillian's. This pool hall, bar and restaurant is a great place for couples. You can kick back and play a couple of games of pool, and enjoy appetizers, pizza, burgers, etc. while you are relaxing. A main feature of this upscale billiard parlor (which covers 2 floors) is the original bar from the old Algonquin Hotel in New York City. The general decor compliments the elegant bar, with green carpet, brass and mahogany trimmings throughout. The crowd ranges from ages twenty-one to thirty-plus (you must be over twenty-one). There is lots of background music and conversation, but it never gets so loud you can't talk to each other.

The dress is casual to after-work clothes, depending on the time and the night. Jillian's does have a dress code, however, so no baseball caps, cut-off shorts or jeans with holes. Pool tables rent for $5.00 per hour during the day, and $6.00 at night (for table and one person; additional players are $2.00 per person). The maximum your table will cost is $12.00 if four people are playing. Jillian's is open until 2:00 AM during the week, and until 4:00 AM on the weekends. Smoking is permitted throughout the establishment. They accept Visa and Master-Card, but no checks. Beers run $2.75 and up (beer and wine bar only).

2-11 Billiard Club
2304 2nd Avenue
Downtown Seattle
443-1211

Billiards has made a comeback in the past few years. The 2-11 Billiard Club is a popular hangout for both novices and experts. The atmosphere looks like you'd expect: there is nothing pretentious or stuffy about this pool hall. The age range of the players is anywhere from twenty-one to sixty-plus, and there is a definite sense of camaraderie.

The 2-11 club attracts a college crowd on the weekends, and an older, regular crowd during the week. If you are good friends, this is a great way to enjoy a casual evening, playing pool, drinking beer and watching the other games. Tables are $4.50 for two players and $6.00 for three or more, per hour. The 2-11 is open Monday through Saturday from 11:00 AM to 1:30 AM, and from 3:00 PM to 11:00 PM on Sundays. Rack 'em up!

Bowling

A night of bowling can be a terrific evening, whether or not you and your date know much about the game. In most bowling alleys, you can also opt for video games or shoot some pool. All this costs less then a movie, and you can have fun and talk and just generally enjoy each other's company. There are vending machines available for snacking, plus a restaurant and a lounge. With the rapid extinction of bowling lanes in our area, you might want to put this one on your "do it soon" list.

Kenmore 50 Lanes
7638 NE Bothell Way
Bothell
486-5555

Open 24 hours (!), this popular bowling establishment does not have pool tables, but they do have video games, a restaurant, lounge and snack vending machines. The cost to bowl varies slightly with the time of day or night, but runs from $1.50 to $2.70.

Totem Bowl
13033 NE 70th Place
Kirkland (Totem Lake)
827-0785

Open from 9:00 AM to 2:00 AM daily, Totem has video games and a restaurant, lounge and vending machines. Lanes cost $2.50 and shoes rent for $1.25.

Village Bowling Lanes
4900 25th N.E.
University Village
524-4800

Bowling lanes can be rented by the hour: before 6:00 PM they are $7.50 and after 6:00 PM they are $8.00. The shoes are $1.50 per person. The pool tables are $5.00 per hour and video games are 25 cents. The Bistro Restaurant and the Yodel'n Room are available for food and drinks. Village Bowling Lanes are open from 9:00 AM until 2:00 AM, during the summer. Winter hours may differ; call ahead for specific hours.

Sunvilla Bowling Lanes
3080 148th Ave
Eastgate Shopping Center (behind Safeway)
Off I-90 at 150th St. Exit, Bellevue
455-8155

Sunvilla is open from 9:00 AM to 11:00 PM Sunday through Thursday, from 9:00 AM to 12:00 AM Friday and from 9:00 AM to 1:00 AM Saturday. The prices are: $2.70 per game after 6:00 PM weekends and evenings, and $2.25 per game before 6:00 PM Monday through Friday. Sunvilla has a restaurant and lounge, as well as vending machines. Pool tables and video games are available.

Dancing

The Washington Dance Club
1017 Stewart Street
Corner of Stewart and Boren
628-8939

The Washington Dance Club offers lessons plus two evenings of dance open to the public. Admission is $6.00 per person, for an evening of ballroom, swing and Latin dancing. Non-alcoholic refreshments are served. Hours are from 9:00 PM to 11:30 PM on Fridays and from 7:00 PM to 9:30 PM on Sundays.

Although ballroom dancing may appear to be a lost art, the Washington Dance Club offers the following suggestions of other local places to enjoy an evening on the dance floor:

Beso Del Sol (4468 Stone Way N.; 547-8087) provides Salsa/Disco Music on a regular basis. **The Red Lion Hotel at Sea-Tac** (18740 Pacific Hwy S.; 246-8600) **and Bellevue** (300 112th SE; 455-1300) has ballroom and/or swing dances. Call for details. **The Four Seasons Olympic Hotel** holds dancing in the **Garden Court** (see entry for the Garden Court in Chapter 4). **The New Melody Tavern** (5213 Ballard NW; 782-3480) plays all kinds of music, but on occasion plays swing, rhythm and blues or Latin music. **The Seattle Center** (684-8582; 684-7200) also holds ballroom and square dancing regularly.

Gregg's Greenlake Cycle Inc.

7007 Woodlawn NE
Greenlake
523-1822

Whether you are seriously into sports, or just in the mood for a little exercise, Green Lake is the primo urban destination for a variety of outdoor athletic activities. Gregg's Greenlake Cycle Inc. rents bikes, rollerskates and rollerblades by the hour. You can race around the lake, or take your time and enjoy the scenery. Either way, you get to enjoy being outdoors, being together, and watching the interesting "traffic" around the lake. Both the bikes and the skates are only $4.00 per hour. You will need a Washington State driver's license to leave with Gregg's, so be prepared. Gregg's rents from 9:30 to 7:30 PM every day, and the last rental goes out at 7:30 PM. Renting outdoor equipment is dependent on the weather, so check your forecast before making this date! For more information call Gregg's at 523-1822.

Note: Paddleboats are available for rent through the concessionaire at the Green Lake Boathouse from April 1 to September 30 (527-0171).

Husky Football

Husky Stadium
University of Washington
Phone: 543-2200

Football fans rejoice when football season is back. If you are a couple who loves the game, why not make a date to cheer on these Rose Bowl champs with the one you love? A Husky Football game and tailgate picnic is one of the most popular ways to spend a fall Saturday

In Seattle. Why not join the crowd? For your tailgate, you can pack a romantic picnic, or bring subs and potato chips.

There is one catch, these Husky tickets sell out very fast. In fact, the tickets go on sale as early as March, so you must buy them in advance if you want to be sure to see the game. If you are lucky, you may know someone with season tickets to share or sell. The box office is open from 8:30 AM to 4:00 PM, and closes at 5:00 PM on Fridays. Tickets cost approximately $20.00.

Ice Skating

Highland Ice Arena
18005 Aurora Ave. N.
North Seattle
546-2431

Take a date ice-skating any time of the year at the Highland Ice Arena. Dress in warm clothes and cuddle up, slowly circling the rink, or turn it into a sporting event and go for the gold. The rink is open year round, but the summer hours are different than winter.

Summer daytime hours: Monday-Friday 10:00 AM to 12:15 PM and 2:00 PM to 4:00 PM, Saturday 10:00 AM to 12:00 PM and 1:30 to 4:45 PM, Sunday 10:00 AM to 12:00 PM and 2:00 PM to 5:00 PM.

Summer evening hours: Wednesday 8:00 PM to 10:00 PM, Friday 7:30 PM to 11:00 PM, Saturday 8:00 PM to 11:00 PM and Sunday 7:00 PM to 9:00 PM.

Winter hours: (starting August 31) Monday-Friday 10:30 AM to 12:30 PM and 3:00 PM to 5:15 PM and Saturday 1:30 PM to 4:45 PM.

The charge is $4.00 for adults, $3.50 for children twelve to seventeen, and $3.00 for children six to eleven. Skate rental is $1.50 for each person. There are snack machines located in the lobby if you get hungry.

Lynnwood's Sno-King Ice Arena
19803 68th Avene W.
Lynnwood/Edmonds border
775-7511

The newly remodeled Sno-King offers a wide variety of skating sessions: public "open" skate times, lessons, "sticks and pucks," and figure skating competitions. It's best to call their information number before you make your plans, as sessions do change frequently. The cost is $4.00 per person (all ages); skate rentals are $2.00.

Ronald McDonald House Ice Rink
The Seattle Center
Winter holiday season only

For the skating schedule of this popular seasonal rink, call the Seattle Center Information number: 684-7200. The proceeds from your admission ticket go to Ronald McDonald House. The rink is only open during Winterfest at the Seattle Center.

The Mountaineers Club
300 3rd Avenue West
Lower Queen Anne
284-6310

The Mountaineers Club offers great opportunities to couples who live in the northwest because they love the outdoors. There's an extremely active singles group, but you are also welcome to bring a date along to any of the many activities. (Note: If you are a steady couple, you will both be required to join after a few times. The single fee is $39). The club puts on dances where you don't need to be, or even know, a member.

By joining the club, you can enjoy a broad range of guided activities: hiking, canoeing, folkdance, climbing, bicycling, outdoor photography, sailing, snowshoeing and more. As a member, you can invite a guest to any of the various events. How many dates have you taken snowshoeing? The club provides introductory to advanced opportunities for you and a friend, or spouse.

For more information on joining the Mountaineers call 284-6310; the office hours are from 8:30 AM to 6:30 PM. There are also information meetings at 7:30 PM on the first Wednesday of every month.

Northwest Outdoor Center
2100 Westlake North
West side of Lake Union
281-9694

An outdoor adventure can make for a great Northwest-style date. Why not rent a canoe or kayak? Northwest Outdoor Center rents canoes, kayaks and double kayaks by the hour. Paddling around Lake

Union any time of day is scenic and interesting. At sunset, the lake can be very romantic. Bring a picnic and the day is complete. You can also dock at one of the popular lake-side restaurants for a beverage or a bite to eat. Rental hours are Monday through Friday, 10:00 AM to 8:00 PM and Saturday and Sunday, 9:00 AM to 6:00 PM. Costs are: $5.00 for a canoe/per hour, $7.00 for a kayak/per hour and $9.00 for a double kayak/per hour. Northwest Outdoor will give you any advice and instructions necessary before you head out, and they supply flotation devices.

UW Canoe Rentals

SE corner Husky Stadium Lot (off Montlake Blvd)
University of Washington campus
543-2100

A canoe for two can be extremely romantic, just plain fun, or a bit of both. The University of Washington rents canoes and it's an easy paddle to and around the Arboretum's waterways. Pack a picnic and go at sunset, or spend a sunny Saturday playing in the water. The boats must be in by 8:30 PM, but that still gives you time for dinner under a tree, by the water. You need a valid driver's license to rent the canoe, so be sure you bring one along. The UW requires, and provides, flotation devices. The canoes are rented out of the Waterfront Activity Center, which is located below the Stadium (enter through the West Plaza entrance). The Waterfront activity center is open weekdays from February 8 to October 31st. Hours are 10:00 AM to 8:30 PM weekdays and weekends from 9:00 AM to 8:30 PM. Canoe rentals are $1.60 per hour for UW students, and $3.50 per hour for anyone else. Bon voyage!

Zone's

2207 Bel-Red Road
Bellevue/Redmond border
746-9411

Zone's is an indoor amusement park for all age ranges. The giant game room includes miniature golf, video games, pool tables, batting cages, air hockey...you get the picture! The miniature golf features a Pacific Northwest theme: the Pike Place market, a ferry boat and Microsoft, to name a few. The age range is from eight to eighty-plus! No matter how old or young you are, you'll have fun. Though Zone's can be loud, and often crowded, you'll be so busy with the games and the surroundings, you won't mind.

Miniature golf is $4.00 for individuals and $3.50 for groups of four or more. Four quarters will get you twelve pitches at the batting cage and the video games are a quarter. Zone's has a cafeteria stocked with hot-dogs, pizza, soft-drinks and espresso (about $1.00 to $8.00). The hours are from 11:00 AM to 10:00 PM, Monday through Thursday, from 11:00 AM to 12:00 AM on Friday and Saturday, and from 11:00 AM to 8:00 PM on Sundays.

B̲e cool. And even if you aren't, you probably want to know where those who are spend their time. Special correspondents Jason Stotler and T.J. Hanify literally worked day and night to verify the politically correct appropriateness of taking a friend to any of the following places. The choices run from mild (a cup of coffee at an all-night diner) to how-wild-would-you-like-it? Seattle has always been known for keeping vanguard music and coffee houses alive during the more conservative eras. Some of you will be glad to know they are still thriving.

B&O Espresso

Cafe/Coffee House
Belmont and Olive Way
Capitol Hill
322-5028

Mon-Thurs 7:30 a.m. to Midnight
Fri 7:30 a.m. to 1:00 a.m.
Sat 9:00 a.m. to 1:00 a.m.
Sun 9:00 a.m. to Midnight

An oil lamp on your table (probably next to a vase of flowers) adds to the glow of other lighting fixtures so the room is dim but not dreary. The surrounding furnishings and interior design create a pleasing sense of informal elegance. The tables are fairly close together, but the clientele is usually more interested in their own affairs than yours.

An idle comment about some of the art on the wall eventually leads to a full-blown conversation about the mysteries of life. Having just finished off a delicious piece of cake, you take a sip of coffee and glance at the far wall—the one with all the posters announcing upcoming events. And you spot one for that play you really want to see. The two of you decide that it would be perfect for your next rendezvous. Your heart skips a beat, and you wonder where you'd be if I hadn't told you about this place.

In addition to being an ideal environment for romance, B&O Espresso also offers breakfast (waffles, pancakes, omelettes, French toast) and lunch (soups, salads, quiches, sandwiches, "American" and Mediterranean style on pita bread). Daily specials, too. And then there's the desserts and the coffee/espresso options. Espresso prices: $1.00 to $3.15; dessert prices: 75 cents to $3.00. The B&O only accepts cash payment.

The Backstage

Food/Drinks/Live Music
2208 NW Market
Ballard
781-2805/789-1184

21 and over

Open until 2:00 a.m.
Shows start at 9:00 p.m.

The Backstage, an impressively spacious tavern in Ballard, is hidden a floor below street level. The large bar always has room for a few more, and dinner is also available. (reservations recommended). They accept major credit cards and checks.

The Backstage is a fine place to see a show and often hosts major talent in a variety of musical styles. It's recommended that tickets be purchased in advance (usually available through Ticketmaster or in person at their box office Monday through Friday from noon to 5:00 PM). Ticket prices generally run from $6.00 to $12.00, with a discount for advance purchase.

Though basically casual, the dress style as well as the average age, varies depending on the style of music being offered. In any case, the Backstage is never stuffy, and the friendly staff makes sure that all over 21 feel welcome.

The Ballard Firehouse

Food/Drinks/Live music
3429 Russell Avenue NW
Ballard
784-3516

21 and over

Dinner every day 5:30 to midnight
Bar until 2:00 a.m.

Here's a surprise: this tavern is in Ballard and was once a firehouse. The Ballard Firehouse hosts a restaurant, fully stocked bar and a small stage which features local rock talent several nights a week. It's loaded with "olde tavern" atmosphere and is a fine place for just dinner or drinks, if a show's not in order. It's easy to spot the tall, unusual architecture of this building on the corner of Russell and

Market. If you just go for dinner, you can order Italian specialties and pizza priced from $6.00 to $10.00. The bands play at 9:30, and the cover charge varies with the group. The Firehouse accepts major credit cards, but no checks.

Beth's Cafe

Classic Diner
7311 Aurora N.
782-5588

Open 24 hours

Beth's Cafe on Aurora would be one of the best-kept secrets in town, if only so many people didn't know about it. It's hard to understand the beauty of this diner without experiencing it. Beth's is: a jukebox full of the best and/or worst music of the past four decades of rock n' roll; a hangout; a classic-style diner with good food and hot coffee 24 hours a day. There are thousands of customer-drawn crayon masterpieces on the walls. Breakfast is served anytime: all-you-can-eat hashbrowns, legendary 12-egg omelettes, burgers 'n fries. You'll see smiling happy faces sitting on vinyl seats and leaning over formica tables. In a word, it's America, really.

Cafe Paradiso

Coffee House
1005 E. Pike
Capitol Hill
322-6960

Sun-Thurs until 1:00 a.m.
Fri & Sat until 4:00 a.m.
Mon-Fri open at 6:00 a.m.
Sat & Sun open at 8:00 a.m.

Cafe Paradiso is a slight variation on an old theme. The paint-dabbed walls, the surreal/abstract oil paintings, and the cornucopia of mismatched, antiquated furniture all smack of the coffee houses of the 60's. It's the perfect meeting place for the young artists, musicians, writers, performers, and expatriates of the future. It almost passes for a cafe from the golden age of counterculture, but something gives it a decidedly 90's tone. Perhaps it's the post-punk twenty-something crowd that has made Paradiso their stomping ground. Perhaps not. Regardless, people from all walks and stages of life will actually feel very welcome here.

The Paradiso menu consists of fairly standard, albeit tasty, cafe fare (coffee, espresso, tea, juice, bakery items). If you can stand sitting with those politically-incorrect social castaways known as smokers, I recommend sitting upstairs. Ample space, plate glass windows, and a sloped ceiling give the second floor both a cozy and an open-air feeling. The Paradiso takes local checks, but no credit cards.

Caffe Minnie

Restaurant
101 Denny Way
Where Denny divides Queen Anne and Belltown
448-6263

Open 24 hours

Caffe Minnie is one of the more popular 24 hour cafes in the city. As many have discovered, its location just north of Belltown makes it the perfect place to go after a full night of club-hopping. In the wee hours, it has a devoted following of hip, twenty-something nightowls, but like any good restaurant, its clientele covers the full spectrum of ages and backgrounds.

The decor is fairly straightforward (nice furniture, movie star memorabilia, photos of old Seattle). Some of Minnie's appeal is the upscale, casual tone that makes you feel you are in a nice environment, but not one that requires you to dress up.

The menu offers a dazzling array of pasta, steaks, veal, burgers (regular or vegetarian), seafood, chicken, salads, appetizers, etc. Beer and wine are also available. And only Minnie offers keen pop-icon breakfasts: omelettes named after Frank Sinatra, Lana Turner, Rudolph Valentino, etc.

Round all that off with generous portions, reasonable prices, and a friendly staff, and you've got one heck of a 24 hour diner. (Major credit cards and checks accepted.)

The Crocodile Cafe

Bar/Restaurant/Live Music
2200 2nd Avenue
Second Avenue & Blanchard
441-5611

Food:
Tues-Thurs 7:00 AM to 10:00 PM
Friday 7:00 AM to midnight
Saturday 8:00 AM to midnight
Sunday 9:00 AM to 3:00 PM

Bar:
Tues-Sat 11:00 AM to 2:00 PM

21 and older

Definitely a rising star among the new generation of live music bars, the Crocodile houses a bar, dining room, and showroom, all in separate areas. This way, if you choose to skip the live band, you can still enjoy the bar and restaurant without paying a cover.

A lot of money obviously went into designing the Croc. The colors and furniture are attention-grabbers, and the walls are adorned with objects ranging from local art to stuffed reptiles. The menu was being revamped and expanded as we went to press, but we trust the restaurant alone should continue to be reason enough to stop by.

In addition, however, the fully-stocked bar (hard alcohol, beer, wine, ale) makes this a perfect watering hole for the twenty-something crowd, and the showroom plays host to some of the best local and national alternative rock acts around. Although the two are not connected, drinks can be purchased from waitresses in the showroom, where the stage can be clearly seen from any table in the room.

A full night, replete with dinner, cocktails, and live music, is waiting for you at the Crocodile Cafe. (The Croc will take your Visa or MasterCard, but no checks.)

Cyclops Cafe

Cafe/Restaurant
2416 Western
Belltown
441-1677

Sun-Thurs open until midnight
Fri-Sat until 3:00 a.m.

If seven surrealist painters typed seventy words a minute for seven-hundred years, would they recreate the entire works of William Shakespeare? Probably not, but they might come up with the skewed-50's-suburbia interior design motif of the Cyclops Cafe. With its stucco walls, kooky color scheme, retro furniture and semi-kitsch knick knacks, the Cyclops is a definite feast for the eyes. And if you're hungry in the more conventional sense, the Cyclops will also please your stomach. The menu consists of near-exotic health-oriented meals, and with plenty of daily and weekly specials, it's virtually ever changing. Beer and wine are available. If you're looking for a quirky yet comfortable atmosphere, extra-friendly service, and "food that's good and good for you," the Cyclops is just your place. (Cash only, please.)

The Doghouse

Restaurant
2230 7th Avenue
Downtown Seattle
624-2741

Open 24 hours

Downtown Seattle's living legend, the Doghouse, is the necessary antithesis to those adorably sterile, neon-laden, watered-down, retro-nostalgia, pseudo-diners that tried to be all the rage a few years back. Late night diner enthusiasts are already aware that "all roads lead to the doghouse (where friends meet friends)," but for those not in the know, it's a must-try.

Having served Seattle since 1934, the Doghouse is indisputably the king of round-the-clock-eats. Why, you ask? First off, for sheer authenticity, it can't be beat. The only thing out of place in this timeless/timewarp environment is a jukebox that plays C.D.'s instead of records, but other than that, it's pure mid-twentieth century Americana from floor to ceiling. The cuisine is classic, too (steaks, seafood, sandwiches, breakfast combo's) as are the beverages (beer, wine, soda, coffee and a full cocktail bar). For background music, plug some quarters in the jukebox or head into the lounge and dig the piano stylings of Dick Dickerson (Wed-Sun, 9:30 PM to 1:30 AM).

Meals are ordered from and delivered by some of the nicest waitresses in town. The Doghouse even has pull-tab machines for those of you still on speaking terms with Lady Luck. I'll stake my literary reputation that the clock outside says it's "time to Eat," at this very moment, so what are you waiting for? (Cash only, please.)

The Grand Illusion

Cafe & Movie Theater
1403 & 1405 NE 50th
University District
523-3935/525-9573

Mon-Thurs 8:30 a.m. to 11:00 p.m.
Fri & Sat 8:30 a.m. to 11:30 p.m.
Sun 8:30 a.m. to 10:30 p.m.

We don't actually know anyone who has a small cinema/cafe in their home, but visiting the Grand Illusion is kind of like walking into a familiar living room. The decor probably has something to do with this sensation. The framed art, persian rug and glass-top tables create a "home-sweet-home" atmosphere that is topped off by the comfy "antique" couch in front of the fireplace. Just outside, there's a large deck with seating for warm summer nights. The cafe serves breakfast (Monday-Friday 8:30 to 11:00 AM), lunch (Monday-Friday 11:30 AM to 3:00 PM) and brunch (Saturday, Sunday 8:30 AM to 2:00 PM). All meals are based on a health-food menu. At times other than these, you can choose from a variety of beverages and baked goods (which are terrific, but may not exactly meet the aforementioned health-food criteria). The Grand Illusion accepts cash and personal checks, but no credit cards.

The appeal of the theater, just a few steps away, is its intimate size and penchant for films you won't see at the profit-hungry multi-plexes. (See page 28 for details.)

The Last Exit

Coffee House
3930 Brooklyn Avenue
University District
545-9873

Mon-Thurs 7:00 AM to midnight
Friday 7:00 AM to 2:00 AM
Saturday 11:00 AM to 2:00 AM
Sunday 11:00 AM to midnight

Seemingly left over from the 1960's (mainly because it is), the Last Exit on Brooklyn is, in fact, Seattle's oldest coffee house. "Leave behind the fast pace of the street," and enter a building teeming with atmosphere. On its own, the furniture would appear very plain: basic, wooden, utilitarian. However, under the soft, but ample, lighting of hanging glass lamps, the tables and chairs exude an aura of coziness. Paintings by local artists float motionless in a sea of antiquated earth-tone-floral-print-wallpaper. Anybody who every dug Jack Kerouac should feel at home here. (Note: although smoking is allowed in designated areas, the restaurant is not very large, and smoke travels quickly.)

The menu consists mainly of sandwiches, soups and salads, but you'll have a difficult time making up your mind. Choose from almost 30 sandwiches, ranging from roast turkey to meatball trailers to the "red sockeye salmon salad sandwich." As for drinks, a wide variety of teas, coffee, espressos, juices and Italian sodas are available. The Last Exit accepts cash only.

On Monday nights, beginning at 9:00 PM, the Last Exit welcomes "open music." This is a kind of amateur night where you can hear everything from classical to folk, and a lot in between!

There's no need to rush off after finishing your meal or beverage. The Last Exit is perfect for relaxing, talking, people-watching, or maybe even planning a revolution. I'm sure it's not easy being the Last Bastion of an era gone by, but someone's got to do it.

ThE Off RAmp

Cafe/Bar/Live Music
109 Eastlake Avenue
Seattle/Montlake Area
628-0232

21 and over

3:00 p.m. to 2:00 a.m.
Shows start at 9:00 p.m.
Cafe closes at midnight

The Off Ramp derives its name from its somewhat hard to find location tucked away near the Stewart Street off-ramp downtown and almost underneath I-5. To get to it, take the Stewart exit, veer left at the stoplight, and you're there within a block.

The Off Ramp's showroom is separate from the cafe and bar, so it's possible to stop by and enjoy dinner or drinks without paying the cover charge. Live music, usually showcasing local alternative rock acts that make up the much-heralded "Seattle Music Scene," is featured seven nights a week. Monday night is new music night, with most bands playing their first shows.

The dark, cozy bar is reason enough to visit the Off Ramp. Usually populated by a "black leather jacket" crowd, yet low key and neighborhood, it's a popular meeting place for the downtown 21 to 35-and-not-counting crowd. Happy hour runs until 10:00 PM, and drink specials are offered Sunday through Thursday nights. The Off-Ramp accepts Visa and MasterCard, but no personal checks.

The cover charge ranges from $4.00 to $7.00, but can go higher if a big name band is playing. In such cases, tickets are usually sold through Ticketmaster.

The Off Ramp seems to always have a special event in progress. In addition to new music night, there's Ladies' Club night on Tuesdays, Games Night on Wednesdays, and Musician's Club night on Sundays. Also after every show, from 1:00 AM to 2:00 AM, the Off Ramp hosts "Hash after the Bash," the city's greatest drunk-driving deterrent. Basically the audience is bribed into staying put for a while with a 50 cent breakfast (eggs, hashed potatoes, a roll, and coffee). Anyplace generous enough to give this trick a try deserves a visit.

RKCNDY

Bar/Live Music
1812 Yale
Downtown Seattle
623-0470

21 and over

9:00 p.m. to 2:00 a.m. unless otherwise posted
Cover charge varies; call ahead.

"Rock Candy" is one of Seattle's newest bars that caters to the rapidly growing local music scene. It's the largest venue downtown and hosts many touring acts whose audiences wouldn't fill a theater or arena capacity.

RKCNDY also has dance club nights with Seattle's top two D.J.'s. M.C. Queen Lucky hosts "Queens Night Out," which is an evening of Gay disco on Mondays, and Sunday night is "Funk Palace," with rap and funk music delivered by D.J. Riz.

Covered in Graffiti Art Murals, RKCNDY is a big cement bunker of a building that holds a large showroom, a pool room, two bars, an upper balcony, and plenty of space just for wandering around. However, it's not exactly an ideal place to just mellow out at the bar, so if you're heading down to RKCNDY, plan to see a show or dance. They do not accept credit cards or checks; cash only.

Thε Rε-Bar

Bar/Dance Club/Live Music
1114 Howell St.
Downtown Seattle
233-9873

21 and over

Daily 9:00 p.m. to 2:00 a.m.
Except opens 8:00 p.m. on Thurs

The Re-bar is a fashionable dance club with a beer (nine on tap) and wine bar. It caters to both a straight and gay crowd, so no homophobes, please. It's best known as a discotheque, with occasional live music performances. The crowd is generally young and fashion conscious, but varies somewhat depending on the theme of the night.

The decor is always eye-catching, and changes every three months to make sure no one gets too used to it.

Monday is "7 beats per minutes" featuring new dance music, or live music. Tuesday features live alternative music. Wednesday's theme is "World beat music" with a D.J. from K.C.M.U. FM. Thursday is "Queer Disco," with a predominantly gay crowd, and Friday is alternative dance music. Saturday is hosted by M.C. Queen Lucky, who spins the hottest disco hits of the 70's, while Sunday is "Disco Sucks" night with rock/dance songs.

The Re-Bar is an excellent place for dressing up and finishing a night on the town. The crowd is fun and frolicsome, and although they're mostly in their twenties, all should—and will—feel welcome. The cover charge is usually around $3.00 (no cover on Sunday). The Re-Bar only accepts cash. Don't forget to stop at the Photo Booth.

Stella's

Italiano Eats
4500 9th NE
University District
633-1100

Open 24 hours

There's nothing particularly offbeat about Stella's. It's just one of the best restaurants around and it happens to be open 24 hours a day. Located in the belly of the Metro Cinemas, Stella's is a favorite among pre- and post-show moviegoers. Other than that, the clientele runs the gamut from families to college students to twenty-something hipsters to hungry insomniacs to...you get the point.

As soon as you walk in the door, the going gets good: a huge glass display case shows off an impressively large variety of the day's dessert specials. Sit in one of the three split levels or grab a stool at the counter, where you get a behind-the-scenes look at the preparation of your soon-to-be-delicious meal. Relax with a beverage (coffee, soda, beer, wine, cocktails). The upbeat decor is appropriately red, white, and green color scheme plus stained wood trimmings and movie posters. The staff goes our of their way to help make Stella's the "Best 24 Hour Italian Joint in Town." Stella's accepts major credit cards and checks.

The Underground

18-and-over Club/Music/Dancing
5418 NE University Way
University District
547-8412

Wed from 10:00 PM to 3:00 AM
Fri from 10:00 PM to 6:00 AM
Sat from 10:00 PM to 5:00 AM

Sometimes it's hard to tell if the music at dance clubs is for dancing or just to serve as an aural backdrop for the attitude-'n-fashion shows that seem to pervade this particular societal subset. The Underground is no different, of course; it doesn't really matter since that's half the fun anyway. For $6.00 apiece, you and your companion can shake it to Seattle's hippest mix of alternative, techno, acid house, industrial, and gothic music—or you can pick up tips on the latest (anti-)fashion trends months before they show up on the newsstand. The decor is basically a black and white color scheme with highlights of...black...and white.

There's plenty of room off the bi-level dance floor to sit and watch the video screens which play various multimedia film clips. Other than that, you could play in the side room, or perhaps enjoy some snacks from the snack bar (sorry, no alcohol). The Underground is an 18-and-over club, usually drawing in the early to mid-twenties crowd. Note: they only accept cash.

University Coffee

Coffee House
1312 NE 45th
University District
634-3766

Mon-Fri from 6:30AM until 9:00 PM
Sat 7:30 AM to 10:00 PM

Over the past few years, Seattle has become almost synonymous with coffee. Unfortunately, the rise of popularity gave birth to a nasty glut of second-rate espresso outlets. You can pick up a mocha just about everywhere these days: fast food joints, convenience stores, gas stations, and probably even some automated bank machines soon. But where can you and your friend go for an honest caffeine fix? University

Coffee, located just off "the Ave" is, as proprietor Joey Kline puts it, "A good place to get a cup of coffee."

The friendly staff can meet all your beverage needs, whether you prefer the old standbys (mocha cappucino) or your own ridiculous creations ("single, tall, skinny, decaf latte with vanilla," "Eightball," etc.). The low-key, unassuming environment of this shop makes it a perfect warm-up or precursor to a full-fledged date, or just somewhere to stop on the way to a movie, play, concert, etc. University Coffee also serves Italian sodas, juices, tea, pop, and some baked goods (biscotti, butterhorns and the semi-legendary, somewhat enigmatic Uncle Seth's cookies). If you're looking for fine refreshment without the cafe elitism ("you actually drink *drip* coffee? How passè!") put this place on your list. They accept Visa, MasterCard and checks.

The Vogue

Bar/Dancing/Live music
2018 First Avenue
Belltown
443-0673

21 and over

Open daily from 9:00 p.m. until 2:00 a.m.

Once the "grande dame" of the Seattle Scene, the Vogue has had to deal with the arrival of several newer, larger clubs. However, it still remains fiercely popular as a dance club. Monday nights have pre-recorded reggae. Tuesdays and Wednesdays feature live alternative music, with shows usually starting around 10:00 PM. Thursdays are "Ladies' Nights" (free for women, usual charge for menfolk). Fridays and Saturdays are pre-recorded dance music nights, and Sundays host "Leather Thoughts," a fetishistic maelstrom of dancing, drinking, fishnets and black leather. The usual cover charge is $5.00. The Vogue does not take checks; they will take credit cards at the bar.

The Vogue's long, thin and dark interior is reminiscent of New York's infamous club, CBGB's. Though it seems small at the entrance, it stretches back quite a ways, with a long bar lining one side. As far as drinking and dancing go, the Vogue is a Seattle legend.

About the author

Amadeus Mephisto was born in 1971, on the brink of the metric revolution. At age 5, having seen his early years being referred to as "that eccentric proto-punk, neo-beatnik artiste kid," he deiced to join mainstream society and changed his name to the more pleasant moniker, Jason Stotler. No one is quite sure what Stotler was up to for the next decade, but it is known that it had something to do with bad taste in clothing and music. Obsessively protective of his artistic integrity, Stotler has never let any of his work be published (he says it would be "selling out."). Thus, his contribution to this book is the first chance for the general public to experience Stotler's trademark style, which hard-core literary fans have been praising for years as "bland and uninformed." Stotler is currently wrapping up work on his memoirs, aptly entitled *When Did You Guys Stop Liking Grape Soda?*

Jason Stotler wishes to acknowledge his friend and mentor, T.J. Hanify, whose invaluable assistance (i.e., actually writing several of the entries) made it all possible.

8

Walking Together

By Stephen R. Whitney

	1	2	3	4	5
6 *birdwatching in Bellevue*	8	9	10	11 *make the sunset at South Bluff*	12
13	14	15	16	17	18	19
20 *Waterfront Trail bring binocs*	21	22	23 *Green Lake with The Gang*	24	25	26 *sunrise/ breakfast at Leschi*
27	28	29	30	31		

Walking is perhaps the oldest couples activity. In fact, at one time it must have been just about the only way for couples to get away from everyone else. Today, at least in Seattle, walking is one of the most popular types of dates, regardless of age, whether the couple is single or married, or whether the date is the first or five hundredth.

A Word on Walking

The popularity of date walks in the Seattle area is hardly surprising. The area tends to attract folks of outdoorsy bent; its incredible collage of mountains, forest, islands, saltwater, lakes, streams, and cityscape provides an unsurpassed backdrop for pedestrian pursuits; and its excellent network of parks and trails offer walks for every age and taste.

For first dates, a walk, either by itself or combined with a meal or movie or whatever, can't be beat. For starters, walking is by nature more casual than other types of dates. It's a date where both parties can pretend they aren't really dating. You know, we're just walking. Nothing really on the line. Just an opportunity to get acquainted in a non-stressful setting.

Second — let's face it — walking is cheap, and isn't it nice to know that two people can get together to do something fun, without spending a fortune? Third, walking suggests that you are vastly more complex and sensitive than all those other potential partners your date could be spending time with. Finally, walking is a good way to burn off nervous first-date energy, a soothing alternative to fidgeting or rattling on about your roommate or whatever.

For long-time couples, whether single or married, walking remains a rewarding, no-hassle, low-budget, energizing way to connect. When you're walking, you can talk or be silent, as your mood dictates. No one expects you to entertain while you're walking, especially not your mate.

Date walks, of course, must be romantic, depending on your definition of romance. If that definition includes slogging, sweaty browed and burdened like a mule, up the side of a mountain (and why not?), we recommend turning to one of the several excellent hiking guides to this region. But if romance for you means sunsets, city lights, salt air, and mountain views, all with clean shoes and no blisters and a pace suitable for hand holding, then the walks described in this section are for you. The walks described below are either in or near Seattle, and those that are out of town are close to outlying restaurants and other attractions for the romantically inclined. All are easy, more or less level, jaunts that are suitable for people of all ages. Those which are wheel-chair accessible are noted below. Hand holding, of course, is optional.

Distance and Pace

The distances given for each walk are one way, unless noted otherwise. Double the figures to calculate the distance of a round trip. Why, you ask, aren't round-trip distances given in the first place? Because you don't have to walk the entire length of a route. You can turn around a third of the way, a half of the way, or whatever. So, the total, round-trip distance will be different for each couple. Providing the one-way figure makes calculating that total easier.

If time is a factor, use the following table to estimate how much time you'll need:

Pace	Distance Covered In One Hour
Leisurely	1.5 to 2 miles
Normal	2.5 to 3 miles
Brisk	3.5 to 4 miles
Fast	Please, not on a date! You're missing the point.

A Note on Shoes

Most of the walks described below are suitable for street shoes. On a couple of the walks, you should really wear athletic shoes to spare both your feet and your dress shoes. The shoe rating for each walk is noted below.

Finally, let's get real about high heels. They're engineered for showing off women's legs, not for walking. So guys, if you plan to go for an after-dinner walk, tell your date so she can choose whether to bring along her walking shoes. If she chooses not to, save the walk for another time. And gals, give yourself a break. If you must wear high heels before or after your walk, at least take along a second pair of shoes for the pedestrian portion of the evening. Or suggest, tactfully of course, that it might not be the best idea to walk around Green Lake before attending Aida.

Alki Beach

Join the young and restless along Seattle's only stretch of waterfront that feels like a real beach, you know, like they have in Oregon and California. The sand, the classic beach cottages, and the pervasive smell of saltwater, sunscreen, and deep fried cooking all combine to persuade us that we are in Florence, Bandon, Half Moon Bay, Laguna, or countless other seaside resorts between Astoria and San Diego. This is the spot for the midsummer bronze-body beach date, in which case you can walk barefooted the entire length of the beach from Duwamish Head to Alki Point. Or come here after dinner, as the sun is setting, and look west to the purpling Olympics and east, across Elliott Bay, to the towers of downtown Seattle. Or come by day and join the beautiful bodies who are sun bathing, cruising Alki Ave., eating, hanging out, and watching one another. To reach Alki Beach, take the West Seattle Freeway to Harbor Ave. S.W. and drive north around Duwamish Head to the beach. Park wherever you find room. Wheelchair access. Street shoes okay.

Distance: 2 miles one way.

Myrtle Edwards Park and Elliott Bay Park

Myrtle Edwards and Elliott Bay parks together form a narrow strip of glory extending northward along the Seattle waterfront for about a mile and a quarter from the public parking lot where Alaskan Way turns left onto Broad Street. No one pays much attention to where one park ends and its neighbor begins, but the official boundary is roughly opposite Thomas Street. The paved path passes public sculptures, benches for foot resting and view gazing, fitness stations, and a fishing pier en route to its northern terminus at 16th Street, near the Port of Seattle's Ellis Island for Japanese automobiles. On a clear day, face the Olympics as you head north, and Mt. Rainier and downtown Seattle as you return south. The fishing pier is a good turnaround for northbound walkers, and if you time your excursion carefully, you can watch the sun set over the Olympics from one of the several benches on the pier. The parks are close to the restaurants and other attractions of the lively Lower Queen Anne neighborhood and only slightly farther from the Pike Place Market and downtown. Except on the warmest days, figure on taking a jacket. This area is consistently windier than almost anywhere else in town. Wheelchair accessible. Street shoes okay.

Distance: 1.5 miles one way.

Magnolia Bluff

From Magnolia Bluff, the view westward across the Sound to the Olympics, and south to downtown Seattle and Mt. Rainier, is so outstanding that this essentially neighborhood stroll draws people from all over town, especially on summer evenings for the sunset show. The elegant houses facing Magnolia Boulevard (for that matter, throughout this affluent neighborhood) provide a visual bonus in the form of beautiful, manicured gardens, which achieve an overwhelming climax of color in April and May, when the rhododendrons and Azaleas are in bloom. Except on the warmest summer days, you are likely to need jackets for this often windy blufftop walk. To reach Magnolia Bluff, drive Elliott Avenue West and follow signs to Magnolia. Cross the Magnolia Bridge and follow W. Galer to a stop sign. Turn left on Howe St., cross a bridge, and shortly veer left on Magnolia Blvd., which curves south, then swings west to the edge of the bluff. Park along the street or in the parking lot at the viewpoint. Walk north or south along the bluff as whim dictates. Northward, the road veers away from the edge of the bluff in about one-half mile, a good place to turn around. More ambitious or preoccupied walkers can continue past posh estates and fine homes to Discovery Park, just over a mile north of the viewpoint. Wheelchair accessible. Street shoes okay.

Distance: 1 mile one way.

South Bluff

Seattle abounds in outstanding places to view the sun setting over the Olympics, but Discovery Park's South Bluff is the ultimate romantic, blow-the-top-of-your-head-off sunset viewpoint in town. Add a ferry or two, or sailboats tacking in the twilight, and the two of you may just swoon straight away. Since South Bluff occupies the western most point of land in all of Seattle, the rest of the city doesn't intrude between you and the vastness to the west. And since South Bluff is accessible only to those who are willing to walk about a half mile from the Discovery Park's South Parking Lot, your companions will be people who are as dedicated to sunsettery as you, and there will be fewer of them than at the more popular roadside viewpoints. What's more, South Meadow, which stretches back from the bluff, is so vast that you won't have much trouble finding a place to yourself. Finally, the natural surroundings, free of autos, houses, and roads, complement the view as no other locale in Seattle can. To reach South Bluff, drive 15th Ave.

N.W. to W. Emerson, just south of the Ballard Bridge. Follow W. Emerson past the Fisherman's Terminal to Gilman Way. Turn right and follow signs to Discovery Park. A couple of blocks before the east entrance to the park, turn left on 34th Ave., then turn right on W. Emerson (yes, you're back on Emerson again) and drive along the south boundary of the park to the entrance to South Parking Lot. From the parking lot, follow the Loop Trail back along the entry road and onward to South Bluff. Restrooms are located at the bluff. Come early to claim a bench at the edge of the cliff. Or follow the Loop Trail a short way beyond South Meadow to South Point, where log seats and a bench await. Walking shoes recommended.

Distance: .5 mile one way.

Green Lake

Green Lake is Seattle's finest and best-loved all-around urban walk. The sunsets are better at Myrtle Edwards Park or Magnolia Bluffs, the body exhibit is more ample and varied at Alki, the view of sound and mountains is far better at Discovery Park. But no walk in town so perfectly blends the combination of urban pleasures and natural beauty. And no walk within a day's drive of Smith Tower offers better people-watching. Everyone walks, runs, roller-blades, or bikes around Green Lake at one time or another, including the most famous names in town — TV personalities, politicians, and sports stars. On a warm summer weekend, it seems like half of Seattle is walking around the lake, while the other half lounges on the grass watching them go by. You can combine a walk around Green Lake with dinner at one of the many fine nearby neighborhood eateries. Or you can make the lake itself the focus of your date. Either way, you can't miss. To get to Green Lake, exit I-5 at 50th, 71st, or 80th streets. Head west and follow your road map to the lake. Parking is available along the street or in one of the three parking lots around the lake. Head for the water and follow the paved two-lane trail clockwise around the lake. Park regulations, which are printed in fading white letters on the trail, state that walkers should proceed counterclockwise, and skaters and bicyclists counter-clockwise, around the lake. This bureaucratic attempt to make the walk safer and saner for everyone may be the most universally ignored regulation in the city. Wheelchair accessible. Street shoes okay.

Distance: 2.9 miles.

Waterfront Trail

The Waterfront Trail makes a perfect evening walk following dinner in the University District or a visit to the Museum of History and Industry. Beginning at the northeast corner of the museum parking lot, a splendid boardwalk meanders among willows, cottonwoods, cattails, and water lilies along the southern fringe of Union Bay, on Lake Washington. Ducks and geese mosey through the marsh; swallows swoop and dive overhead; great blue herons stand motionless, knee deep in water, waiting for hapless frogs. Gaze across Union Bay to Husky Stadium, the University boat house, and Laurelhurst. On a clear day, the Cascades form a spectacular backdrop across Lake Washington to the east. Best of all, from the dating point of view, are the secluded benches located at the end of short side-trails along the way. The trail proceeds about one-half mile to Foster Island, where you can either turn around or continue southward along a broad path into the University of Washington Arboretum. To get to the Waterfront Trail, drive state 520 west to the Montlake exit. At the stoplight on Montlake, continue straight ahead on E. Lake Washington Boulevard for one block, turn left on Park Drive, and continue to the parking lot behind the Museum of History and Industry. From the East Side, drive 520 to the Lake Washington Boulevard exit. Turn right at the stop sign and continue to Park Drive. Wheelchair accessible. Walking shoes recommended.

Distance: .5 mile one way.

Azalea Way

The University of Washington Arboretum is Seattle's largest woodland garden, combining native vegetation with ornamental trees and shrubs from around the world. Numerous trails meander through the Arboretum, following woodland glades, gently ascending to overlooks, winding through forest, and visiting secluded pools and small brooks. Any one of them, either by itself or combined with other activities, makes a great date walk. The Japanese Garden (see entry page 7), with its authentic handmade tea house, makes a splendid stop along the way, especially in autumn, when the Japanese maples are brilliant scarlet, crimson, and orange. The Arboretum saves its most spectacular display of color, however, for spring, when its extensive plantings of rhododendrons and azaleas burst into bloom, beginning in early April and extending through the first week in June. In normal years, this two-month riot of color reaches its climax in early May along Azalea Way, a gentle, grassy lane beginning at the Arboretum Visitor's Center and heading south for perhaps one-half mile. The sheer exuberance, abundance, and variety of color verges on the unbelievable. For the ultimate spring date walk, work off your Sunday brunch with a hand-in-hand stroll down Azalea Way. Prepare to swoon. To get to Azalea Way, drive state 520 west to the Montlake exit. At the stoplight on Montlake, continue straight ahead on E. Lake Washington Boulevard and, in about one-half mile, turn left on Foster Island Road. Wind around to the intersection with Arboretum Drive. Either park here, or continue on Arboretum Drive to the Visitor's Center and more parking. Azalea Way begins across Arboretum Drive from the Visitor's Center. Ask for directions if you get lost. From the East Side, exit on Lake Washington Boulevard. Turn left at the stop sign, immediately left again on Foster Island Road, and proceed as described above. Approaching the Arboretum from the south, follow Lake Washington Boulevard to Arboretum Drive and keep right to the Visitor's Center. Walking shoes recommended.

Distance: .75 mile one way.

Lake Washington Boulevard

The perfect walk for a dawn date, but also great in the early evening, when the sun's last rays turn the glass towers of downtown Bellevue, across the lake, into pillars of fire. In October and November, enjoy one of Seattle's finest displays of fall color. In April and May, marvel at the multihued displays of azaleas and rhododendrons in the manicured yards that line Lake Washington Blvd. On a clear winter day, gaze at the white Cascade crags arrayed along the eastern horizon. In summer, stop along the way to dangle your feet in the lake. If you love the roar, the crowds, the Blue Angel acrobatics, and the roostertails of the hydroplane races, take this walk on Seafair Weekend. If you don't, take it on any other weekend but that one! All year long, watch geese, sailboats, people, and the infinite moods and shadings of Lake Washington. Begin at Seward Park and walk north to Leschi and Madrona Park-or vice-versa. Either way works. Attractions along the way, from north to south, include Madrona Park, the shops and restaurants of Leschi, the current and former I-90 bridges (the latter notable for its absence), Stan Sayres Pits, and Seward Park. Do all or part of it as the mood strikes and as time and energy allow. From Seattle, drive northeast on Madison St. to Lake Washington Blvd., then turn right (south) and follow the sharply winding road to Madrona Park. Or follow Boren and Rainier avenues south to Gennessee St., then turn left (east) and continue to Lake Washington Blvd. From this intersection, you can see Seward Park across Andrews Bay. Head south on Lake Washington Blvd. to the parking lot. Street shoes okay.

Distance: 5 miles one way.

I-90 Bridge

On a warm, clear, day, walk across Lake Washington on the safe, broad pedestrian-bicycle lane perched above the traffic on the north side of the new I-90 bridge, which connects Mercer Island to Seattle. Look south to Boeing, Renton, and Mount Rainier, and north to the Evergreen Point Bridge and beyond. Unless you have a boat, this walk is the best way to experience the great size and beauty of Lake Washington. And it is required therapy for west- or east-bound commuters who barely look at the lake as they hurtle, teeth clenched and eyes glazed, across the bridges each morning and afternoon. This route is mostly the domain of bicycles, so keep right and stay alert. Most riders coming from behind will alert you to their approach with an "On your left." One true precaution: avoid this walk during storms, when high winds and driving rain can pose a hazard, mainly in the form of hypothermia, to pedestrians. From the Seattle side, pick up the route at the junction of 35th Avenue S. and S. Irving. Parking is available on the street. Or you can park below the I-90 bridge on Portal Place and walk up the steps to the entrance onto the bridge. From the Mercer Island side, park in the public parking lot on W. Mercer Way, immediately north of the freeway. The paved path runs along the south side of the parking lot. Wheelchair accessible. Street shoes okay.

Distance: 1 mile one way.

Lake Hills Green Belt

Bellevue's Lake Hills Greenbelt is a narrow corridor of fields and woods extending from Larsen Lake in the north to Phantom Lake in the south. The Greenbelt is a short way from restaurants and other attractions in the Crossroads and Overlake areas, and not much farther from downtown Bellevue. The trail is broad, well maintained, and easy on the feet. Wildlife is plentiful; you may even spot bald eagles working their way up and down the greenbelt from nests near Lake Samammish.

In season, you can buy blueberries from the active blueberry farm surrounding Larsen Lake, and corn from the produce stand near the parking lot at the junction of 156th Avenue S.E. and S.E. 16th Street. From this parking lot, you can walk either south to Phantom Lake or north to Larsen Lake. Or you can park at the Larsen Lake parking area, located on 148th Avenue S.E. between Main Street and S.E 8th Street. Walking shoes recommended.

Distance: 1 mile one way from Larsen Lake to Phantom Lake.

Mercer Slough Nature Park

Located a couple of miles south of downtown Bellevue, the Mercer Slough Nature Park is an excellent place to walk any time of day or year. The park extends north-south on both sides of Mercer Slough, a narrow channel linking Kelsey Creek and Lake Washington. This natural park, combining, marsh, woods, blueberry fields, and meandering channels, currently contains 5 miles of trails, with additional miles to be completed by the end of 1992, and more yet on the drawing board. Existing trails consist mainly of boardwalks, woodchip paths, and paved walkways. By early 1993, a new bridge should cross Mercer Slough, linking the Overlake Blueberry Farm on the west with the old Bellefields Nature Park on the east. For now, the two best walks are the Bellefields loop and the boardwalk beginning at the Sweolocken Canoe Boat Launch, on Bellevue Way, just north of I-90.

From the parking lot at the boat launch, follow the boardwalk south toward Lake Washington, then turn left and walk across and above the wetlands to 118th Avenue S.E. Or drive south of S.E. 8th Street onto 118th Avenue S.E. and continue one-half mile to the small parking lot on the right, near the entrance to the old Bellefields Nature Park. From this parking lot, you can either follow the path that heads southward, parallel to the road, or you can follow the loop trail that begins a few yards south of the parking lot, plunging downslope through woods into the heart of the wetland. Since the Mercer Slough Nature Park trail network is currently under development, be sure to check with the Bellevue Parks Department Ranger (451-7225 or 455-6881) for the latest information on which trails have been completed and are open to the public. Wheelchair accessible. Walking shoes recommended.

Distance: 0.5 to 5 miles, depending on your route.

About the author

Stephen Whitney is author of *Nature Walks in Around Seattle* and *A Field Guide to the Cascades and Olympics.* He currently works as a technical writer for the Microsoft Corporation.

Staging The Perfect Picnic
by Barbara Holz Sullivan

9

Handwritten calendar notes:

- Radar Park Picnic: bring berry pail
- picnic for 2 our secret garden
- "dinner cruise" on the Halewa
- explore NOAA
- Kubota w/ Bentos and Books
- (don't forget lunch)

Many couples whose paths cross in the Northwest never forget the romance of the place. In the Pacific Northwest, you are blessed with themes and elements that exist nowhere else—at least not in the particular interpretations and combinations found here. Whether you've at last met that intriguing someone who suggests the two of you spend more time together, or are part of a long-term pair in search of precious time away from the daily grind, consider a picnic. Show your sensual, spontaneous, fun-loving nature...plan a picnic.

About Picnics

A picnic's casual pace allows you to focus on the place and the food and each other. It allows you the quiet and time to explore mutual interests. If it's your first picnic, it can become a memory that both of you will always associate with the birth of your relationship. If it's your 100th and counting, you can activate all those memories. Your only task is to be ready to take advantage of the area's festive foods and perfect picnic spots—food and places made for romance and memories.

Filling a basket with Seattle's choice foods will not be a problem because you'll each have your own picnic favorites to contribute. It's choosing the perfect spot for your outing that will take a little more thought. It's not a choice to be made cavalierly. The place has to possess significance without being overwhelming. To make it easier, choose from among the following ten couple-tested picnic destinations. The list is a mixture of city gardens, quiet water-views, and lofty vistas, each chosen to inspire a particular theme for your picnic and to be experienced in whichever season love blossoms or seeks renewal.

The Rose Garden at Woodland Park Zoo

5500 Phinney Avenue N.
Seattle
684-4800

Just to the south of the zoo and behind high walls and wrought iron gates, you'll step into Guy Phinney's 1890s tea garden—a quiet, intensely fragrant rose bower. One hundred and ninety species representing every rose hue imaginable are planted in ornate, manicured Victorian splendor. If you can talk your companion into donning vintage clothing, so much the better.

Because there are no tables here, choose picnic foods that are easy to eat with your fingers or from your lap. Benches are scattered among the sculptured shrubbery and reflecting ponds and you can picnic on one of them, or spread a picnic rug if you prefer the plush lawn. The heady fragrance will reach you wherever you sit.

Then, after your picnic, gather the wind-blown petals at your feet to make potpourri or pressed rose beads.

Directions: From I-5 take the NE 50th Street exit and drive west. The south entrance of the zoo is located at North 50th and Fremont Avenue North.

Chateau Ste. Michelle Winery

14111 NE 145th Street
Woodinville
488-1133

You'll have no trouble creating a French theme for this romantic picnic destination. Approach from either side via foot or bike and the Burke-Gilman Trail (which traces the Samammish River to the east and Lake Washington to the west). Bring bread, Brie, and fruit in your basket, or, if you wish to appear spontaneous, purchase pâté and a bottle of wine at the gift shop. Everything you need for a picnic is available there.

Choose a shaded spot on the lawn, then lean back and imagine that the chateau and its grounds are yours. You might even wish to include pad and pastels to create a truly French Impressionist memory of your outing among the vineyards.

Mature trees and flower beds border wandering paths, fountains, ponds, and grassy spots, creating outdoor "rooms," the largest of which is the outdoor amphitheater. In summer, Shakespeare and jazz play to romance and picnickers under the stars (see page 5 for additional details).

Directions: From I-405, take Exit 23A (SR 522, Monroe-Wenatchee) to the Woodinville exit. Turn south (right) off the exit and continue three blocks to NE 175th Street. Turn west (right) and follow the road to the stop sign. Turn south (left) on Hwy 202 and drive approximately two miles to the winery entrance.

NOAA Grounds

7600 Sand Point Way NE
Seattle
526-6385

For an unobstructed, unpopulated, and inspirational water view of Lake Washington, bike or stroll along the Burke-Gilman Trail to NE 70th Street, and down to NOAA (National Oceanic and Atmospheric Administration) property and its collection of outdoor art. Cinder paths cut across wetland grasses and sanctuaries for waterfowl, and through and among sculpted berms and piers and a sound garden built to capture and play windsongs. It's a wondrous place, perfect for the quiet exploration of your relationship.

Except for quick-stop stores on Sand Point Way, there are few places to obtain picnic ingredients nearby, so plan to pack your picnic before starting out.

Directions: From I-5, take the NE 65th Street exit. Drive east on NE 65th Street to Sand Point Way NE. Turn north. Enter the NOAA gate and park near lot 1.

Foster Island

2700 24th Avenue East
Museum of History & Industry
Trail begins in parking lot

Lily pads, slanted sunlight, graceful willows, and journey by canoe lends an impressionistic air to this urban island across the ship canal from the University of Washington stadium. Pull your canoe up onto the bank and unload your feast. Whether you spread a blanket on the grass or find one of the two benches unoccupied, as they often are, you will enjoy a prime view of passing yachts and sailboats through the Montlake Cut. (See Chapter 6 for canoe rentals.)

After you've finished eating, you can stroll along the Waterfront Trail to one of the private view spots. You never know just what or whom you'll encounter as you head across the boardwalk, so be prepared for adventure. One day it might be a beret-topped juggler, the next day a pair of nude sunbathers on a hidden side platform. It's that kind of unforgettable place.

Directions: Located just north of Hwy 520 and the Washington Park Arboretum. The Museum of History and Industry is located two blocks east of Montlake Boulevard. The trail begins in the northeast corner of the parking lot.

Meridian Park

Meridian Avenue N. and N. 50th St.
584-4081

West of the University of Washington, in the heart of Wallingford, is a grand old building complete with weathered gazebo, estate-sized lawn, gnarled orchard, and funky gardens. These and the arched entrance on 50th and Meridian foster a Secret Garden sort of atmosphere which surrounds the former Good Shepherd Home.

Besides the vast expanse of lawn and its orchards, you'll be able to explore and learn from the labeled and scarecrow-guarded Tilth and P-Patch gardens. Chances are, even on a sun-drenched day, you will have the park to yourself. But if you time your picnic to correspond with the annual sales and fairs held by Tilth and others on the grounds, you'll be able to purchase edible plants and take advantage of the bountiful harvests. However, you'll no longer be alone. You choose.

Directions: From I-5, take the NE 50th Street exit and drive west. Turn south (left) on Meridian Avenue North and park on the street.

Radar Park

SE Cougar Mountain Drive
Bellevue
296-4932

Because very few picnickers wend their way to this small, incredible park with its million-dollar view of Lake Samammish, it will seem as if you are the only couple in the whole wide world. In fact, because Radar Park is located high above Bellevue on Cougar Mountain, it will seem as if you're on top of the world. It's a good feeling when you're attempting to initiate a good, solid relationship or get away from the cares below.

Radar Park is worth exploring no matter what the season. Toward the end of summer, you can gather wild black raspberries and red huckleberries and in winter, because of its high elevation, you can carve angels in the snow or attempt to identify the small animal tracks.

Directions: From I-90, take Exit 11-A. Head south on 150th Avenue SE to SE Newport Way. Turn east (left) and follow Newport Way to 164th Avenue SE. Turn south (right) and follow the road up the mountain to Cougar Mountain Way. Turn east (left) and follow the road as it curves to SE 60th Street, turn south (right) and drive one block, then right again at SE Cougar Mountain Drive. Drive approximately 3/4 mile to Radar Park's entrance gate. Park in the lot across from the lone house.

Carl S. English, Jr., Botanical Garden

3015 NW 54th Street
At Ballard Locks
783-7059

In days past, you could have imagined hopping aboard a flatbed by Myrtle Edwards Park and riding it as far as Golden Gardens, or hopping off just the other side of the ship canal for a picnic at the locks. In today's world, you'll have to arrive at the locks by car, foot or bike (or maybe roller blades). You can gather picnic items as you journey past the Redhook Ale Brewery pub or at one of Ballard's Scandinavian food shops.

Once you arrive, head for the terraced banks overlooking the continual parade of water traffic motoring through the locks. But don't assume that the gardens only encompass the area bordering the walk or overlooking the canal. Walk to the west and you'll soon come upon your own unclaimed spot. There you can dream of hopping trains bound for the Far North or barges to China, or...

Directions: From I-5, take the North 85th Street exit. Follow 85th Street west approximately three miles to 32nd Avenue NW. Turn south and drive 1 1/2 miles to NW 54th Street and the entrance to the locks.

The Washington State Ferries

Colman Dock, Pier 52
Seattle
464-6400

Embark on a dreamy adventure I call, "In the Night Ferry" (with all due apologies to Maurice Sendak's popular children's book, *"In the Night Kitchen")*. Start by consulting the newspaper for the posted sunset times, then park your car under the Alaskan way Viaduct and walk onto the Bremerton ferry at the Colman Dock.

Crossing the Sound to Bremerton is one of the longest of the Washington State ferry runs, giving you ample time to open your basket, spread and enjoy its contents, and still stand at the outside rail to catch the crepuscular rays shooting from the setting sun.

On the return crossing to Seattle, you'll be able to witness the gradual lighting of the Seattle night skyline, the end to a perfect picnic.

Directions: Located at Pier 52 on Alaskan Way. From I-5, follow the signs to the "Ferry Terminal."

Kubota Gardens

Corner of Renton Avenue South and 51st Avenue South
Seattle
684-4081

A tranquil, Zen-like quality envelops you as you walk down the path into Kubota Gardens, one of Seattle' newest city parks. At the foot of the hill, stones cross the first pond to a miniature island and its stone lantern. A path on the other side leads over a mound and through the trees to a view of a second pool where a crimson bridge and, in summer, yellow irises cast their rippled reflections. On the other side of the bridge, there's a winding path to the highest point of the park. On the way to the top, you'll encounter boulders carved with Japanese characters. Perhaps they and the imperial water view will inspire you to compose your own Haiku for the occasion.

Flat stones, carved benches, and grassy knolls provide several serene spots for you to celebrate the changing seasons and to share bentos (boxed picnic lunches, Japanese style).

Directions: From I-5, take the Swift Avenue/Albro Place exit. Head south and east on Swift Avenue South (it becomes South Myrtle Street) to Martin Luther King, Jr. Way South. Turn south (right) and drive one block to Renton Avenue South. Turn east (left)) and drive one block past 51st Avenue South to Lindsay Place. Turn south (right) to the park.

Gene F. Coulon Park

1201 Lake Washington Blvd. N.
Renton
235-2560

What if you're looking for romance during a season of cold, damp, and shortened days? What then? Do you have to abandon all thoughts of private picnics in the park? Not at all. Instead, head for one of the area's best kept secrets and create a true Northwest tradition—an Eddie Bauer-REI style, winter picnic.

This best-kept secret is to be found on the southeast corner of Lake Washington in Renton. There, in Gene F. Coulon Park, you will find a large covered pavilion with a central firepit, perfect for cozy, toasty picnics in the middle of December.

What could be more romantic or relaxing than the glow of embers reflected in your smiles and eyes, than the licking of melted marshmallows from your chilled fingers, than the lapping of the waves and the dripping of the rain from the roof? Trust me: a winter picnic in the Northwest becomes one the two of you will never forget.

Directions: From I-405, take the NE Park Avenue and Sunset Blvd. NE exit and head west toward the lake. Follow the signs to Coulon Memorial Park and turn north (right) on Lake Washington Boulevard North.

About the author

Barbara Sullivan is the author of *Seattle Picnics: Favorite Sites, Seasonal Menus, and 100 Recipes* from Alaska Northwest Books. She lives in Seattle with her husband and four children, where she proved that in Seattle is possible to meet, date, and marry that special someone.

Sullivan was born in Dubuque, Iowa and has worked as a nurse in Minnesota, Pennsylvania, and Missouri before moving to Washington. During her many moves and travels, she has collected food and family lore.

Currently she is Coordinator of Learning Resources at Seattle University School of Nursing where she puts her love of computers to use.

Suggested Companion Guides to
Stepping Out In Seattle

Breakfast in Seattle

Where to go for the first meal of the day in and around Seattle
by Marilyn Martin Dahl and Kay Vail-Hayden
Photographs by Larry Dahl
JASI Publications

Just Italian!

A Guide to Italian Restaurants in and Around Seattle
by Merilee Frets
JASI Publications

Nature Walks In & Around Seattle

All Season Exploring in Parks, Forests & Wetlands
by Stephen R. Whitney
The Mountaineers

Seattle Picnics

Favorite Sites, Seasonal Menus, and 100 Recipes
by Barbara Holz Sullivan
Alaska Northwest

Index

Subject Index

Mandy Johnston is an English Major and Political Science Minor from the University of San Diego. She grew up in Bellevue, and has been a Northwesterner since she was two. Mandy enjoys the outdoors as well as the ballet and movies. Other interests include drawing, acting and reading. Her best dates always include a romantic cup of espresso and good conversation.

This is Mandy's first book, but as the daughter of Priscilla Johnston, author and publisher of *The Seattle Super Shopper*, she has guidebooks in her veins.